Thank you so much for purchasing my book!
I'm excited to see you accomplish your
goals with what you learn in this book.
If at any point while reading this book, you'd like to
receive a free marketing consultation, just scan the QR
code below to book a call with one of my team members:

Praise for "Marketing Magic"

If you want to learn the art of marketing, read this book. The goal of marketing is to capture attention and convert that attention into sales. Manuel can show you how to do it. Read this book cover to cover, implement what you learn and enjoy more customers and more sales in your business!

-Ezra Firestone
Founder smartmarketer.com

***

I own many companies, some making billions of dollars in revenue. I sit on the Board of Directors of international firms. I meet all kinds of people, and I boil them down to two types: those TALKING about doing great things and those actually DOING great things.

I have known Manuel for many years, he doesn't just talk about making it, he IS making it. He has created some of the most successful people on the internet. The TOP spots on Amazon, YouTube, you name it. I have seen him bring companies back from the dead; companies that should have died but are now breaking all-time records.

There are many people out there selling ideas, but few, if any, are the Genius Manuel is.

But I am biased. I became so impressed and so blown away by Manuel's marketing powers, I just had to buy part of his company. So, you just need to buy his book.

-Tom Cummins
CEO/Founder of American Power and Gas
& Global Gas and Light

***

I've been in the trenches as a successful entrepreneur for over two decades. In that time, I've started and built numerous multimillion dollar businesses, including the world's most successful e-commerce coaching business. I've crossed paths with literally thousands of students and fellow entrepreneurs, yet there have only been a few instances where a student has gone on to achieve such a high degree of success and influence, like Manuel has achieved! My experience has shown me that very few people possess a unique ability to learn a business skill, put it into practice, get results, and then effectively teach others how to achieve similar success. I've observed Manuel's NaturalSlim® brand and his marketing agency reach remarkable heights, and over the years, he has become a good friend. He understands his marketing business, delivers results, and knows how to teach well. So, pay close attention to this book. It might be precisely what you need to excel in the business and marketing game. HIGHLY RECOMMENDED.

- Ben Cummings
Founder of Elevated E-commerce
BenCummings.com

***

Manuel is one of the greats. He has a perfect blend of marketing genius, leadership, big vision strategy and ethics which is why his success continues! Every time we catch up, he's working on amazing new projects and his companies keep growing rapidly. If you are looking to get both inspiration and marketing breakthroughs, Manuel and his content is a perfect next step! Don't sleep on what he's doing, what he has to say, and how you can use it to transform your life! Get ready for breakthroughs and transformations!

-Rudy Mawer
Celebrity Marketer & The Man in Red

Founder of MawerCapital.com, TheRedLife.com & ROIMachines.com

***

I knew Manuel when he was just getting started, before he built the empire he has today. He was just as genuine and kind then as he is now. But he was tenacious in growing his abilities and understanding of marketing and business. His rapid growth has been incredible to watch. I don't care whether it's marketing, advertising, content, leadership or any other aspect of business, there hasn't been much Manuel hasn't mastered. You would be dumb to ignore anything he has to share.

- Dan Henry
Founder of closedeals.com and getclients.com

***

Manuel Suarez has helped me widen my scope of helping others. If you want to help a few people, then great, but if you want to help the masses, read this book.

- Dr. Eric Berg
"The Knowledge Doc"

***

I first had the idea of working with Manuel Suarez back in December of 2019, before the world completely went upside down. Until then we had been working on a pretty modest marketing operation. I had a weekly CEO briefing that I wanted to popularize and in addition, we wanted to properly advertise for investments in the company and its products.

I clearly remember the conversation we had right around Christmas. Manuel was gung-ho to get going, even though it was clear then as now, that we were a comparatively small client.

So, we got going and in short, the transformation of our marketing was instantaneous. I found that the AGM® team, while still developing many of its features such as content, was highly professional and responsible.

We have since brought our marketing in-house and have brought amazing new talent to do so, therefore reducing our reliance on outside agencies. But for us, Manuel and his team, AGM® agency, really helped us experience and create a new paradigm that was closer to my experience as a marketing exec myself.

I think that Manuel's main trait is an extraordinary amount of caring and interest, combined with a great deal of energy and speed. That's true of all great execs, such as Steve Jobs, who would famously reduce someone's 90-day project to three weeks! That is essential for the head of any organization and Manuel has not only done that himself but has attracted extraordinary people to his team to do that along with him.

AGM® is also at the forefront of technology innovation, right now playing with AI and its potential which is unlimited but still very, very immature. Companies and personalities that are fortunate enough to be serviced by AGM® agency do extremely well and I think that it makes AGM® and its leader among the foremost marketers in the country – and possibly the world.

-Riggs Eckelberry
CEO of OriginClear and Water on Demand

How I produced 7 billion views, 50 million social media followers and $250,000,000 in yearly revenue without paid advertising!

MARKETING MAGIC

By The Marketing Ninja MANUEL SUÁREZ

AGM® Press

ISBN: 979-8-218-18894-8

AGM® Press
1200 Starkey Rd Unit 215-A
Largo, FL 33771
United States
Email: info@agmagency.com
Phone: US 1-888-280-3339

To connect with Manuel Suarez:
www.ManuelSuarez.com

Social Media Profiles
Facebook: www.facebook.com/theninjamarketer
Instagram: www.instagram.com/mrmanuelsuarez
YouTube: www.youtube.com/@ManuelSuarezNinja TikTok: www.tiktok.com/@mrmanuelsuarez
LinkedIn: www.linkedin.com/in/mrmanuelsuarez

Printed in Colombia by
Panamericana Formas e Impresos S. A.

DEDICATION

"Marketing Magic" is dedicated to the most important person in my career, my hero, my number one mentor, and my father, the late Frank Suarez; to my beautiful wife and best friend, Gaby Suarez; and to the original source of my inspiration, my four children, Sofía, Julian, Camila, and Adrian.

TABLE OF CONTENTS

WHY "MARKETING MAGIC"

I want to start by preparing you for a potentially life-changing adventure by explaining why I decided to title this book "Marketing Magic." Let's start by defining the two words that make up the title.

MARKETING: *Marketing is the activity, set of institutions, and processes for creating, communicating, delivering, and exchanging offerings that have value for customers, clients, partners, and society at large.*

The above definition is what you'll find on Google, but I'd like to share what it has come to mean to me over the years. But first, let me define another word that you'll see in just a moment:

SUPERPOWER: *An ability to positively influence the lives of others with one's message, products, or services.*

All right, now here's *my* definition of marketing:

MARKETING: *The forming of a brand or a person's Superpower, followed by the development and execution of a strategy for the dissemination and distribution of that brand or Superpower, which in turn leads to captured attention and thus the inevitable expansion of one's purpose.*

Okay, so now that I've defined marketing, let's move on to the second word in the title of this book:

MAGIC: *The power of apparently influencing the course of events by using mysterious or supernatural forces.*

The above is the first definition you'll find when you Google the word "magic". Magic has long been regarded as something "not real," "hard to comprehend," or "a supernatural power or influence only available to a few very special people."

This "supernatural power of influence," this "magic" applied to the subject of marketing is what this entire book is about. My goal is to make it real for you that you too can have a little bit (or a lot) of this "Marketing Magic" that I've been blessed with throughout my marketing career.

I'm going to show you that by applying what you learn in this book, you'll be able to build your own legacy in this ever-changing world of opportunity.

One last thing. I'm on a mission to impact as many people as possible. As you go through this book, feel free to send me questions, feedback, realizations, or simply say hello. If you are in the US, you can reach me by text at 813-212-2196. Or, you can send me a direct message to my Instagram account, @ mrmanuelsuarez.

FOREWORD

By all accounts, I shouldn't be here. I am a small-town Iowa boy clinically diagnosed with ADHD and PTSD. I'm bad at almost everything and only really good at a couple of things. But those few things allowed me to sell hundreds of millions of dollars, break industry records, and impact people from all walks of life, like Manuel Suarez, whose fine book you now have.

Manuel happened to be on a webinar in 2014 where I was selling a product that he decided to buy, even though he was flat broke. Manuel then took that product and, with a lot of his own hard work and ingenuity, went out and reached tens of millions, had content he produced viewed billions of times, and sold hundreds of millions of dollars.

We started where you probably are right now - with little more than a desire and willingness to learn and try out new things. To the outside world, what Manuel and I do looks like magic, hence the book's name. Now you see it (the problems), and now you don't (the fantastic results). It appears that we do the impossible in front of your eyes, so to call it magic makes sense. But the difference is this: most magicians do not reveal their tricks. Manuel does, as you'll see in this book. Manuel and I want you to know the tricks because the better you can succeed with them, the more opportunities it opens up for all of us.

Manuel went from being my customer to becoming a marketing partner in a new venture where we have already sold millions. I also hired Manuel's agency to help me start my social media following since, after 15 years and hundreds of millions of dollars, I figured it was time to get out in public. We both want YOU to succeed because magicians can learn from each other, push each other, and work together to create a greater magic show.

But just like magic - to make it appear effortless, you must put in much effort. Manuel is one of the most on-fire action takers I know of - and I know everyone. Sure, you'll have to practice the magic tricks he shows, but he's made it as easy as possible for you to learn them quickly and increase your chances of succeeding with them sooner rather than later.

Manuel has a hall of fame in his office for people who have impacted him in life and business, and one of the proudest moments in my career was to be a face on his wall of fame. I hope you take this book's contents to heart, put it to work, and get such a great result that you'll put Manuel's face on your wall of fame.

Jason Fladlien
The Webinar King

INTRODUCTION

The purpose of this book is to show you, the reader, in a practical way, how to *execute* the marketing tips and strategies I will share with you here. Over the years, I have put together formulas that I used to accomplish success for every brand I've worked with. To make this book as timeless as possible, I made it a point to include mostly "evergreen" advice for both marketing and the mindset you'll need to make your goals a reality.

What I mean by "evergreen" is synonymous with "timeless." Like an evergreen tree that never loses its leaves, your education here won't change with every whim of the internet. In other words, you won't need to get yourself an updated copy of this book next week because the algorithm changed, yet again, on your favorite social media platform.

This book will give you the basic philosophy that guides me as I create marketing magic for my clients. It's my biggest mission in life to demonstrate to every person I reach, whether through my videos, presentations, articles, or within these pages, the powerful opportunities that every one of us has available at our fingertips.

Speaking of opportunities, more often than not, I'm looking to *leverage existing opportunities* in our environment rather than create new ones. My obsession lies in a never-ending pursuit of *impact*, and the only way this impact becomes an actuality at the largest scale possible is by *observing the obvious* in our environment and *acting* based on these observations. For context, I'd like to tell you a quick story.

My father had a vision. A big one. He wanted to share his incredible message with the world and help millions of Latin American people improve their metabolism, health, and self-esteem. He wanted to create a *massive impact*, and like with any endeavor, he made both correct and incorrect decisions along the way. Let's break them down…

CORRECT DECISIONS

- Use the internet to spread his message.
- Consistently create easy-to-understand educational videos to teach people how to improve their metabolism and health.
- Create a content channel (MetabolismoTV®*) where people can view these educational videos.

  **Inspired by Gary Vaynerchuk's "Wine Library TV."*

WRONG DECISIONS

- Not leverage YouTube or other existing social networks.
- Only upload his content to his own website (MetabolismoTV.com), which he would have to drive his own traffic to via TV ads and other marketing means.

Do you know what happened for the first year or so? No one watched. We ran all types of marketing campaigns – television ads, emails, flyers, posters, banners, and so on; *nothing worked.* He made close to two hundred videos of content without *any attention* for almost an entire year.

Then, one very bright day, after several failed attempts, we were able to convince my father to give us the green light to create a MetabolismoTV® YouTube channel. On that day, March 17th, 2012, the first-ever MetabolismoTV® video was uploaded to YouTube in my home office.

We spent the next few weeks uploading seven to eight videos daily from the hundreds of videos that we already had.

Today, a decade later, this content channel has generated over one billion views on YouTube alone.

Considering the current population of this planet, you could almost say that one person out of every eight has seen one of my father's videos. Of course, this isn't actually the case considering we have many repeat viewers who are "addicted" (in a healthy way) to our content, but it gives you an idea of the impact we've made with this specific content channel. In fact, this channel happens to be one of the largest health-related YouTube channels in the world, and is a big reason why his brand, NaturalSlim® has become a 9-figure international brand.

Now, here's the crazy part: The growth of his social media channels was all accomplished with *zero* advertising dollars. Just throwing that in there to give you a taste of the power of this "marketing magic" I'll be sharing throughout this book.

So, like I mentioned earlier, my dad made his fair share of great and not-so-great decisions that ultimately ended up delaying his success.

If he had been willing to leverage one of the largest search engines on the planet, YouTube, from the beginning, we would have reached our goals and created the impact he wanted to create *faster*.

What can we learn from this story? Opportunities are *always present*, but only for those willing to *look* for them.

In this ever-changing marketing landscape, the most important thing you must do is remain aware of what is happening *now*. Things simply change *too fast*, and if you're not on top of it, it's easy to feel defeated.

However, if you make it a point to always *look* for opportunities, I promise you, no matter what the economy is going through, what the government tells you or what your neighbor says, you will *always find* them.

Maybe it doesn't seem realistic to you now, but this fact will become evident to you as you progress through this book.

HOW TO MAKE THIS BOOK YOUR NINJA SIDEKICK

My goal with this book is that you actively *apply* what you learn here. Therefore, I want you and I to make an agreement first. It involves your decision to study these pages in a way that goes far beyond skimming with mild interest. See if you can agree to the following points:

1. Use this marketing book as your guide for *doing* something, not just for casual reading. Commit to studying every marketing concept with the intention to understand it well enough to apply it to your business and your life so you can reach your own personal and business goals.
2. There will be a few exercises in this book. When you come across one, do it right then instead of waiting until you reach the end of the book.
3. Throughout this book, you may come across words or terms that are new to you. Some of these words might be specific to marketing or business, while others might be common words with multiple meanings. Even if you *think* you know them, make it a point to check out the definitions. Real knowledge comes from truly understanding the material, including the specific words used.
4. Start shifting your efforts and mindset toward the purpose of *helping others*. This one will make more sense

later in the book, but you'll find out soon enough that this trait alone is a key factor for success.

5. Stay in touch. If at any point you have questions, comments, feedback, or anything else, feel free to send me a text at 813-212-2196 (if in the USA), or a direct message via my Instagram account, @mrmanuelsuarez. I may not respond immediately but I promise I'll get back to you!

You may have heard the saying, "You don't know what you don't know." As a marketer, this is a concept I live by, but the idea here is to be curious and always eager to learn. You'll want to have this mindset while reading this book.

LESSONS I LEARNED FROM MY MOST VALUABLE MENTOR

"Your business should be inspired by purpose, not money."
The Ninja Says

Since launching my marketing company, Attention Grabbing Media® (AGM®) just under ten years ago, we've proudly accepted many awards, including three consecutive Inc 5000 awards (in 2020, 2021, and 2022).

Some may only see these accomplishments and not consider what it took to become eligible for them. However, there were multiple elements, including the valuable lessons I learned from my mentors, that paved the way for this to happen in the first place.

Over the years, I've been fortunate to have several amazing mentors in my life, but the most influential of them all was my dad.

I worked with him very closely for years and during that time he shared a few lessons with me that I'll never forget. I believe they are as relevant today as they were when he shared them with me, and I'd like to pass them along to you here:

LESSON 1: "IT'S ABOUT PURPOSE, NOT MONEY."

One of the first lessons my father taught me was that a business should never be just about money; it should be about *purpose*. He demonstrated this throughout his life, and it was clear that he was far more interested in helping others than how many sales were made.

In today's social media-dominated world, the brands that make a significant impact are those that effectively use their Superpower to help others. No matter what type of business you have, it has the potential to improve someone's life.

If you don't have that clear, you're going to struggle. Sure, you might get lucky enough to generate some money, but at some point, that's going to die out if you're not working towards building something that will last for generations. In other words, a legacy.

Within the world of social media, legacy represents the everlasting content you leave behind on digital platforms, immortalized for future generations.

Think about it. Wouldn't it be amazing if we could watch recordings of Jesus' sermons or one of Nikola Tesla's discussions on YouTube? This is the power of building a legacy, especially with the massive communication channels we have available today.

This concept of legacy became very real to me when I lost my father in 2021. His wisdom continues to guide people even in his absence and will do so for generations to come. Thanks to the technology of today, my daughter can watch him and remember the influential figure her grandfather was.

My father is now reaching more people than he did while he was alive, across various platforms. His Superpower continues to help others, even though he's no longer with us. His legacy remains vibrant and alive today. It was never about money for him; it was about purpose and legacy.

LESSON 2: "NEVER SAY 'I SPENT.' ALWAYS SAY, 'I INVESTED.'"

The first time I told my dad I spent a thousand dollars on a Facebook ad, he was quick to correct me. "Listen, son," he'd tell me, "You're not 'spending', you're 'investing'."

His point was clear. In the marketing game, we don't just "spend" money. We're investing *energy*, which is pretty much what money boils down to. We're investing money (energy) to capture people's attention. Whether it's old school media like TV, radio, newspapers, and magazines, or today's social media platforms like YouTube, Facebook, Instagram – the name of the game is getting noticed.

Of course, you have to be smart about where you invest that money. Some investments will be lucrative, while some won't be. Either way, the idea here is that you're *flowing energy* towards something – in this case, attention. Not just "spending" money.

LESSON 3: "IF AN ARM IS BLEEDING OUT, CUT IT AND STOP THE BLEEDING."

My father had an incredible knack for analyzing an organization and spotting the problem areas. He often compared a business to a human body. If a part of the organization, or an 'arm' as he would say, was failing and causing harm to the rest of the body, it should be removed to prevent further damage.

This analogy could be applied to your own business, or life, even. Let's say you've recently added a new product to your beauty brand. Maybe it's a unique facial cream sourced from the Himalayas. You've fallen in love with it, but no matter what you try, it isn't catching on with customers. The demand just isn't there.

At the same time, your other products have continued to do well for some time now, so a portion of the revenue has gone towards funding this other product. So, what now?

My dad's advice would be to follow what's doing well. Avoid causing harm to your whole organization because of a sentimental attachment.

I clearly remember one day when my father shared this piece of wisdom with me. We were at a bowling alley, discussing a new product I had launched for my Cosy House bed sheets brand — a line of bamboo bed sheets. I loved the product, but I was losing money on it every month. "Son," he said, "you need to let it go."

I took his advice to heart and let go of my emotional attachment to it, knowing that holding on would jeopardize my entire brand.

If you look at the histories of successful entrepreneurs, you'll find a common denominator: They typically focused relentlessly on *one thing* for a long period of time, often going through hardships along the way.

So, just to clarify, I'm not suggesting you abandon your goals and dreams. But if you have several products or businesses, and your efforts are not producing results in a particular area, it might be time to make some tough decisions.

Building something of value will inevitably come with its own share of hardship. But that focused attention is what makes the difference. The same goes for trying to juggle multiple ventures at the same time — you're more likely to fail. So, concentrate on the one thing you truly believe in and remove the "waste".

LESSON 4: "A WAR IS WON WITH A STRATEGY."

One of the most important lessons my father passed on to me was the importance of strategy in achieving success. He believed that victory, whether in a war or in business, relied on a well-planned strategy rather than isolated campaigns or battles.

The strategy we used for NaturalSlim® was to leverage my father's expertise and magnetic personality by having him appear daily on MetabolismoTV®, which generated a ton of attention and more customers than we could have ever imagined.

At my marketing agency, Attention Grabbing Media®, we never start a project without having a clear strategy in place. Regardless of the endeavor, you need to be able to visualize the goal, map it out, understand the necessary investment, assign responsibilities, and execute the plan. If the initial plan doesn't yield the desired results, you reassess and repeat the process.

To offer some clarity, I'd like to define what I mean by "strategy" in the context of marketing:

STRATEGY: A detailed, step-by-step plan, encompassing both short-term and long-term initiatives, aimed at capturing attention and fostering the growth of your business. A marketing strategy is typically a written document that aligns your team with the marketing objectives for your products or services. It usually includes the following components:

- Purpose
- Overall brand goals
- The brand's story

- The ultimate value or desired outcome of products and/or services. For example, "To help people improve their self-confidence through better health"
- The messaging, content, and value that the brand or business provides
- Existing assets, including social media platforms, followers, customer and prospect lists, content, etc.
- Products and/or services, with a clear description of each
- Competitor research and analysis
- Any marketing restrictions
- Marketing goals
- Marketing KPIs (Key Performance Indicators)
- Paid ads strategy, including any current opportunities (Staying aware of existing opportunities is essential.)

If you would like to see an example of a complete marketing strategy, scan the QR code below to get access now:

I'm very firm about never launching a marketing campaign or investing any funds without a complete Marketing Strategy in place, which is understood across my agency. This approach significantly improves the likelihood of success. Keep in mind that the digital world changes very quickly, so marketing strategies need to be adaptable. You must be ready to adjust your approach in response to changes in the marketing landscape.

Formulating, outlining, and implementing successful marketing strategies is like becoming a Hall of Fame baseball player. A baseball player who can achieve a hit three times out of ten is often considered worthy of the Hall of Fame. Similarly, in marketing, you may fail seven times out of ten, but if you succeed in the remaining three, you're on track for long-term success.

Throughout this book, I'll share the strategies that brought the brands I've worked with to record-breaking levels of growth.

Remember, no war has ever been won through random action. Victories are achieved through strategic planning.

LESSON 5: NOTHING IS MORE VALUABLE THAN YOUR TEAM.

I could write an entire chapter about this last point. My dad built an incredible team because he knew he couldn't accomplish his big goals without some help. His company (NaturalSlim®), which I now run, is driven by a purpose that he put in place years ago and is now continually kept alive by the team he created.

Admittedly, the idea of having a team has been a personal obsession of mine. I've always been an extrovert and enjoyed having many friends. If you're like me, building a team is the most amazing thing you can do. You end up surrounding yourself with friends, allies, and warriors who transform work from a boring necessity into a fun adventure.

The employees I have at Attention Grabbing Media® and NaturalSlim® are more than just coworkers; they're friends I enjoy spending time with both on and off the clock. I believe that that alone is evidence that you have the right people around you.

I've made it my personal mission to surround myself with incredible individuals who share a common purpose of succeeding personally and professionally. They're not just with me to clock in and out; they're committed to making a difference and being part of something extraordinary. And this is why I'll never forget when my father would tell me again and again, "Nothing is more valuable than your team... a team of dedicated people sharing a purpose."

To recap, here are the fundamental lessons I learned from my father:

1. IT'S ABOUT PURPOSE, NOT MONEY.
2. NEVER SAY "I SPENT." ALWAYS SAY, "I INVESTED."
3. IF AN ARM IS BLEEDING OUT, CUT IT AND STOP THE BLEEDING.
4. A WAR IS WON WITH A STRATEGY.
5. NOTHING IS MORE VALUABLE THAN YOUR TEAM.

These lessons helped guide me throughout my own journey, and I hope they can do the same for you.

CATCHING OPPORTUNITY WAVES

"I make it a point to find opportunities no matter what's happening in the world of social media, marketing, the economy, or elsewhere."

The Ninja Says

My journey began with a single opportunity which changed the course of my life. As you'll soon discover as you read through the rest of this book, the ability to find and leverage opportunities will make you truly invincible. No matter what the state of the economy is or what's happening in the world, you'll never fall victim to the false idea that there's "nothing you can do." Let me share a little about how my entire journey began.

It all started shortly after my wife and I had moved to the USA. She was pregnant with our first child, and although I didn't have a penny to my name, credit history, or evidence that I should be trusted with a $250,000 bank home loan, we were approved for our first mortgage.

Not long after, the subprime mortgage crisis hit, and along with many others, we lost everything.

I can tell you, from the depth of my heart, there's nothing more embarrassing as a man than being unable to care for your loved ones. But that moment is when something sparked inside of me, and I became certain of one thing: I was going to do everything in my power to ensure that we'd never be in such a situation again. It wasn't just about me anymore - my wife and children were relying on me. It was then that finding opportunities became my obsession.

Not long after all of this occurred, my wife suggested the idea of introducing my father's weight loss brand, NaturalSlim®, to the US market. I wasn't completely on board with the idea at first, because I doubted our ability to make it a success. I feared having yet another disappointment, but something inside of me told me to give it a shot anyways and present the idea to my father.

One night, over dinner at a restaurant, we met with my father and pitched the idea to him. After giving it some thought, he agreed and wrote us a check for $10,000 on the spot. With that, NaturalSlim® USA was born.

Fast forward to 2012, despite our efforts with traditional marketing and cold calling, sales were far from ideal. Some months, we only managed to generate a few hundred dollars. But I wasn't giving up yet. It was during this year that we began to crack the code of what I call "marketing magic", and the rest is history.

Today, NaturalSlim® has generated hundreds of millions in sales and has served over a million customers worldwide. In fact, in 2023 it's a 9-figure international brand operating in 9 countries. In the USA alone, it's an 8-figure business that's on track to produce 85 million by the end of 2023.

How I managed to accomplish this is exactly what I'll be sharing in this book, but it all began with a single opportunity.

This experience changed my entire perspective. Instead of life being full of dead ends, I now consider it to be full of possibilities as long as you are willing to look for them. Your mindset can play a big part in this.

For example, a pessimistic mindset will blame social media algorithms for their inability to succeed, while a more optimistic mindset will actively *look* for ways that they can take advantage of these changes. Personally, I make it a point to find these opportunities no matter what's happening in the world of social media, marketing, the economy, or elsewhere.

Whether we like it or not, the world is constantly changing. Sometimes these changes are yearly or monthly. When it comes to social media and marketing, these changes could be weekly or daily, even. This is why you have to be willing to continuously adjust and stay up to date on what's happening *now*.

One of my favorite quotes is by the philosopher Seneca: "Luck is what happens when preparation meets opportunity." The truth is, it's not just about the availability of opportunities; it's about your decision to walk through those open doors. You might one day find yourself surrounded by opportunities, but it's up to you to leverage them.

If my father hadn't extended that opportunity, my life might have taken a different turn. Yet, the fact remains that opportunities are present every single day. All you need to do is keep your eyes open. And as we proceed to the next chapter, I will provide you with a formula to unlock these unexpected opportunities, just as I did.

THE SUCCESS FORMULA

"I truly believe there are endless opportunities."
The Ninja Says

For most of my life, I didn't show any promise of achieving anything great or significant because I honestly didn't believe that I could be successful.

Despite that, just in the past decade, I have reached levels of success I never thought I would experience. Not only was able to grow NaturalSlim® into a 9-figure international brand, but my marketing agency has won three back-to-back Inc 5000 awards, among many others. It's been a dream come true, to be honest.

Through significant personal growth and the decision to leverage opportunities around me, I was able to change my entire life. The best part is that my level of security does not depend on the government or the state of the economy. I am in control of my future, and my goal is to help you get to this point as well, possibly even faster than I did.

After looking at exactly what turned my life around the first time (and has continued to do so), I found that there were three key actions I was doing every time that I successfully took myself to new heights. Let's dive into these.

The first thing I did was put myself in proximity to power by connecting with people who were influential, impactful, successful, and eager for growth. These individuals are dedicated learners, hard workers, and intelligent, as demonstrated by their accomplishments. They have a burning desire to achieve remarkable things, and they are often successful. None of these qualities necessarily had to do with their wealth. It was more of a state of being or a condition of existence.

My first significant encounter with this came in 2008, during the economic crisis that I talked about earlier. At the time, I was attempting to reconnect with my father who I considered an incredible source of power.

Although my connection with him was inconsistent for years, there was a point that I realized that just being connected to him would open the door to opportunities. So, when I hit that "low" in my life, I decided to do just that: reconnect and flow power to that source of power.

Doing this, as you know, led to an opportunity that changed my life forever, and ultimately became a big part of my success today.

As much as I would love to say that these types of opportunities will land in your lap without any effort of your own, that isn't the case. Even having a negative mindset will stop you from finding them.

For example, if you're the type to complain about the state of the economy, how the world is changing, or how challenging life is, opportunities may seem non-existent. You won't even spot them. But by slightly shifting your mindset toward one that is more optimistic, your chances of discovering them increase greatly.

Personally, I truly believe there are endless opportunities and all I need to do is reach out and grab them. I also consider that there is always room for growth, both for myself and the quality of my life.

Now, although the initial opportunity presented to me by my father was the beginning of what changed my life forever, it wasn't until I *acted* on it that it became a reality. This is a very important point. It's not enough to simply recognize an opportunity. You have to *do* something with it.

What took things even further for me was adding value to that power source. In other words, I made it my mission to not only deliver on my promise and produce results, but to give even more than they expected. Doing this is what proved that their investment in me, whether it was time, money, or both, was worthwhile.

To recap, these are the steps that shaped my personal journey toward success:

STEP ONE - Establish Proximity to Power: Position yourself close to influential and impactful individuals.

STEP TWO - Recognize Opportunities: Keep a close eye on the potential opportunities around you.

STEP THREE - Take Action: When an opportunity presents itself, grab ahold of it, add value to it, and deliver on your promises.

Try implementing these steps and maybe you'll find that there are more opportunities around you than you originally thought.

Before you move on to the next chapter, here is a simple exercise I'd like you to do: Find a notepad, either digital or paper, and list out any sources of power available to you. These could be friends, employers, teachers, mentors, family, church members, acquaintances, or anyone that fits the criteria covered in this chapter. Again, you are looking for successful, influential, or impactful people who are dedicated to learning, eager for growth, hardworking, and have a burning desire to achieve remarkable things.

This list will help you identify the potential influences within your surroundings, which is the first step of the process. It might also spark a few ideas on how to connect with these individuals. Think about ways to build on these relationships and remain open to the opportunities each may present.

THE PRIMARY STRATEGY

"Providing value to the world around us remains forever the strongest strategy for both personal and business growth."
The Ninja Says

There is one strategy that has produced the most significant results for my own brands as well as those we help through my marketing agency. The next few chapters will share the details of this strategy.

Tried and tested repeatedly, this strategy stands the test of time because it's rooted in delivering genuine value without any hidden agenda. In fact, as you will soon discover, this concept of providing value to the world around us remains forever the strongest strategy for both personal and business growth.

Here it is:

1. Find out what your Superpower is.
2. Start creating valuable content to share your knowledge and message with the world. Focus on helping others.
3. Use existing channels to share your content.
4. Commit to creating and posting content consistently.
5. Ramp up your efforts by creating and posting even more content on as many platforms as possible.
6. Add fuel to the fire by investing in ads that push your successful content out even further.

7. Start building your list through lead generation strategies.
8. Present your product or service only to those who have benefited from your Superpower via your content.

Are you ready to dive into each of these? Let's go!

DETERMINING YOUR SUPERPOWER

"Your Superpower is your ability to positively influence the lives of others with your message, products, or services."

The Ninja Says

The beginning of the Primary Strategy starts with figuring out what your Superpower is. As covered earlier, a Superpower is defined as, "An ability to positively influence the lives of others with one's message, products, or services."

Identifying your Superpower, to some extent, involves tapping into your interests and strengths. Maybe you have an eye for fashion. Or, you've had a lot of success in helping businesses become more organized and efficient. Perhaps you love gardening and can inspire others to grow their own food.

Just like my father discovered his talent for helping people regain their health and lose weight, and how I uncovered my marketing skills, you too can discover your unique Superpower.

Your Superpower may be something *you* might overlook but could significantly improve other people's lives. It's likely a topic you love talking about, or one that you feel you can provide the most value with to those around you. Even a subject generally considered dull, such as accounting, can save people millions and protect their families, making it a powerful Superpower.

If you haven't discovered your Superpower yet, ask yourself the following questions:

1. What do you love doing?
2. What do you love talking about?
3. What is the message you want to share with the world?
4. How do you or your business help people?
5. What was the reason behind starting your business or doing what you love?
6. What do you consider to be your best abilities?
7. What skills do you have?
8. How can your products or services improve someone's life?
9. Do you love entertaining others? (That's a Superpower in and of itself.)
10. Are others inspired by you? (That's another Superpower.)
11. Are you able to teach people?

If you are a business owner, a great starting point is to look at what inspired you to create your business to begin with.

For example, if you own an organic product business, maybe you were initially driven by a purpose to help others improve their general health and longevity. That's an incredible Superpower that's very needed today.

Or, maybe you created an art supply business because you loved creating art and wanted to inspire others to find their own creativity through art. That's another great Superpower!

To me, a Superpower is an ability that you have that can positively impact someone else's life. You may even take the knowledge and experience you have for granted because it comes so naturally to you that it doesn't seem special. Whether you own a business, have a job that you excel at, or even if you're merely pursuing a passion, there will be some kind of Superpower that drives you.

Even jobs that don't require advanced skills have an ability. For example, someone who works in the fast-food industry for a living might have an incredible ability to multitask and do things quickly. A security guard might have the ability to spot a troublemaker before anyone else can. The difficulty level of a job or passion doesn't determine whether you have a Superpower or not. If you are good at it, there is an undeniable ability present.

Again, a Superpower is an ability to positively influence someone else's life. When you execute this ability, you are using your Superpower! This applies across all industries and areas of expertise. It doesn't matter if you're a realtor, own a niche e-commerce brand, are an accountant, or a writer. You have the ability to positively impact someone else's life in the form of entertainment, education, or inspiration.

People often ask me how I discovered my own Superpower, which has led to the development of a great organization with hundreds of employees. How did I uncover my Superpower?

For me, this discovery was formed over two key moments in my life. The first was during the 2007 subprime market crash in the United States where I lost everything: my home, my job, my income, my dignity. I'll share more about this story later, but it was one of the lowest moments in my life.

The second, a few years later, was during a moment of observation. At the time, my father had already been creating content and delivering seminars to share his knowledge about the metabolism. I was inspired by his ability to impact others, but I also observed a unique phenomenon happening in the world that didn't exist when I was growing up.

What I saw were people looking at their phones and actively consuming content. This was the exact moment I realized that there was something magical about this era. We had an opportunity that our ancestors would have only dreamt of, where the potential audience was not only huge and easily accessible, but the competition to reach them was low. In other words, there were far more people consuming content than creating it, and that alone was a huge opportunity.

It was then that I decided to go all in and leverage this unique opportunity, which was the beginning of the development and realization of my Superpower in the world of marketing. I didn't even know what the word "marketing" meant at the time, but I eventually came to realize that I had been doing it all along, and that I was actually good at it!

Once you discover your Superpower, your next step is to *take action*. Action itself will be the foundation of all your future success. In my case, I realized that marketing was my ability, my Superpower. Today, everything from my social media content to my business revolves around my ability to improve the lives of others through my knowledge of marketing.

To provide you with some inspiration in finding your own Superpower, I'd like to share a few examples of Superpowers of people I've had the privilege to know and work with personally:

FRANK SUÁREZ
(My father)

Superpower:

Frank transformed the lives of millions across the planet through his health education both online and in person. He did this with his profound expertise and unique ability to communicate complicated topics in a relatable manner. His knowledge of the metabolism, obesity, and proper nutrition has helped people regain their power over their health and well-being. Even though Frank is no longer with us, his content is being seen by more people around the globe today than ever before.

Frank himself didn't have a degree from any university stating that he was an authority on the subject. He simply developed a passion for it and decided to dedicate his life to researching the subject and helping other people with the correct information that they could understand, apply, and see results with. He had a unique ability to explain complicated subjects like the human body in a way that anyone could understand.

Total followers on social media as of 2023:
Approximately 22 million.

DR. ERIC BERG

Superpower:

Dr. Berg is a chiropractor who specializes in helping people get healthy to lose weight. He does this by teaching others about Healthy Keto and Intermittent Fasting. He is the author of several books including the best-selling book *The Healthy*

Keto Plan. His supplement brand, Dr. Berg® Supplements, has helped millions of people achieve their health and weight loss goals.

One of the key elements of his unique Superpower is his ability to break down complex health concepts into simple, digestible lessons. He also covers a wide range of health-related topics, from diet to exercise, often focusing on natural solutions.

Total followers on social media as of 2023:
Approximately 16 million.

NANCY CARTWRIGHT

Superpower:

Nancy's main Superpower is bringing joy and entertainment to millions of people of all ages.

For over three decades, she has vocally brought life to iconic cartoon characters on The Simpsons and Rugrats, among others. She is also an accomplished artist and actress both in movies and her comedy skits as Darlene Davenport.

Total followers on social media as of 2023:
Approximately 3 million.

CHICK COREA

Superpower:

Chick had an amazing ability to make playing the piano look as natural as breathing. But more than that, he inspired millions of people to create art in any form. During Chick's musical career, he won twenty-seven Grammys and is the fourth-most decorated Grammy Award-winning artist in history.

Chick had an intense passion for helping others through his music and his teachings. He spent the last few years of his life showing thousands of artists how he accomplished greatness (without ever calling himself great).

I've never met a humbler person in my life in the sphere of music, but mostly I admired how he truly enjoyed being a musician and working on his passion. He made music his Superpower and spent many decades sharing this with the world at large with an abundance of joy. Before we lost him in early 2021, he impacted the lives of many millions of people.

Total followers on social media as of 2023:
Approximately 1.4 million.

JASON FLADLIEN

Superpower:

Jason Fladlien is known as the *Webinar King*. His pitch webinars have set records in the information, coaching, affiliate, and software spaces. Many of today's top marketers, including Russel Brunson, Kevin Harrington, and Alex Hormozi, believe he's the best there is when it comes to webinars. He is also the author of the best-selling book *One to Many* and is considered one of the best teachers on the subject of creating and presenting webinars.

He has helped make hundreds of millionaires by teaching them the art and science of presenting and converting product and service offers through webinars or marketing in general.

He was one of my first mentors and today, he is, without a doubt, one of my primary marketing mentors.

Total followers on social media as of 2023:
Approximately 20,000.

BRANDON DAWSON

Superpower:

Brandon Dawson is a serial entrepreneur who has bought and sold over one hundred and twenty businesses during his thirty-plus-year career. He is a brilliant business mind with incredible knowledge and value. During a recent interview with Grant Cardone, Grant was asked, "What is your greatest regret in life?" His answer, "Not meeting Brandon Dawson earlier."

Recently, Brandon decided to bring that experience and wealth of business knowledge to social media. His goal in doing so is to influence and inspire entrepreneurs and business owners around the globe to grow and scale their businesses. Through his content, he aims to give practical and actionable business advice for both personal and professional development that will help his audience do better in the game of business.

Total followers on social media as of 2023:
Approximately 890,000.

***

Now that you have an idea of what a Superpower is, take this time to answer the questions I listed earlier in this chapter. Look over your own interests, abilities and strengths and see if you can determine your own Superpower.

Once you have that, you can use it to leverage the world of social media and become what I like to call a "Content Unicorn."

BECOMING A CONTENT UNICORN

"A Content Unicorn is a person with an impactful message that has the potential to make a significant positive impact on others."
The Ninja Says

No matter how you might feel about your abilities, knowledge and experience, there are people out there who need and want your help. Now it's up to you to make both yourself and your message known. The people who do this best are what I like to refer to as "Content Unicorns."

First, let's start by defining this term. "Content" is defined as the data, information, value, education, inspiration, and entertainment that appears on the internet or elsewhere, such as a magazine or this book. In fact, this book is a consolidation of a lot of my internet content.

As far as "unicorn" goes, the most well-known definition is "a mythical animal typically represented as a horse with a single straight horn projecting from its forehead", which you'll find on Google. However, there is another definition that is perfect for this concept of a "Content Unicorn", which is: "something that is highly desirable but difficult to find or obtain".

So, with that in mind, here is how I define a Content Unicorn:

"A person who has an impactful message that has the potential to make a significant positive impact on others and has the ability, desire and courage to share their message by leveraging today's communication channels in order to achieve that very purpose."

By this point, it has probably become clear to you that there is still a giant opportunity within the world of content creation. With most people actively consuming content and very few consistently creating it, there is a huge potential opportunity to reach audiences who want or need our help.

Over the years, I've had the honor of working with several Content Unicorns. Besides being "natural" money-magnets, they all had similar qualities that set them apart from the rest. I'll share them here:

1. They are "obsessed" with their industry, passion or skill and feel like they could talk about it forever.
2. They genuinely believe in their message and that it has the power to truly benefit people in some way.
3. They are in it for the long haul and are not in it to "get rich quick."
4. They understand the value of attention. In the online world and social media, this translates to views, followers, subscribers, engagement, website visitors, etc. Although revenue plays a part, they know that the more attention they get, the more they will attract income.
5. They understand the power of content and are very disciplined about creating it consistently.
6. They are willing to be in front of a camera, regardless of whether they consider themselves an introvert or an extrovert. A great example of this is Dr. Eric Berg, a Content Unicorn I have the pleasure of working with, who attended "Fear of Public Speaking" courses to

gather the courage to face audiences. Today, he has one of the largest health-related YouTube channels in the world.

7. They are passionate and dedicated to expanding their knowledge.
8. They are good and ethical people with high-quality products and services.
9. They are more interested in helping others than generating revenue. No disrespect *at all* to revenue creation; that is, after all, what we're going for. But what motivates them more than anything is knowing that they can help others.
10. They are surrounded by a team devoted to the same purpose. They understand that a great team can help them to focus on their greatest strength (their Superpower) and help them forward their overall purpose.

Now that you understand the traits that make up a Content Unicorn, you might feel equally excited and intimidated. Maybe you're worried about whether you can become one. Or perhaps you're thinking you're late to the game.

First, remember this: the Internet itself is only about twenty-five years old, a speck in the timeline of history. There's a good chance that some readers of this book remember what life was like before the internet.

Secondly, it's never too late to share your Superpower with the world. Content creation is an ever-evolving landscape, with new opportunities and audiences emerging daily. Plus, your unique Superpower and your personal journey will automatically set you apart. Your genuine love for what you're passionate about and the depth of knowledge you have will make you stand out, even in what might feel like an oversaturated market.

But remember, becoming a Content Unicorn isn't an overnight transformation. It's a journey, and like any journey, it begins with a single step. That step is recognizing your Superpower, the thing you're passionate and knowledgeable about. You've already completed that step in the previous chapter.

Now, it's time to put that Superpower to use and let it guide you in creating content that resonates with people, answers their questions and helps them improve their lives in some way. As you step into this new phase, keep in mind the qualities of a Content Unicorn that I shared in this chapter. Let these characteristics guide you in your journey.

And if you're worried about being good enough, just know this: you don't have to be perfect from day one. Every piece of content you create, every interaction you have, is an opportunity to learn, grow, and refine your message. Over time, you'll find your voice and your audience.

So, embrace your Superpower, start creating, and remember, the world needs your unique perspective. Who knows? You could be the next Content Unicorn who inspires, educates, and entertains people all over the world. There's a massive playground of opportunity out there waiting for you. It's your turn to step into the game and shine.

MASTERING THE ART OF ATTENTION

"In the world of social media and business, attention is currency."
The Ninja Says

Now that we've covered how to find your own unique Superpower and tapped into the qualities that make a Content Unicorn, it's time to look at how to use those to capture attention.

First, becoming a Content Unicorn is more like running a marathon than a sprint. It needs dedication, constant progress, and a deep desire to help others with your unique message. In this chapter, we'll discuss the steps you need to take to make an impact using today's communication channels. It's time to take action. Let's start at the top:

Step One: Make a commitment to the journey.

Every goal starts with a decision. In this instance, you'll want to begin your journey by deciding to commit to going through the entire process.

This starts with the decision to start but also includes committing to getting through each of the steps it will take to reach your goals.

As I mentioned in the previous chapter, one of the common traits I have observed with every Content Unicorn I have worked with is that they are not only committed to the process, but they are committed to helping and impacting people. They are determined to do whatever it takes to achieve their goals. No matter what obstacles come up, whether it's government-mandated shutdowns, hurricanes, a "failing" economy, or anything else, they continue to create content to share their message with the world. They are fully committed to their message, their content creation routines, and everything needed to achieve their goals.

When you're just starting, you'll have to figure out what you *can* commit to. For example, when it comes to content creation, maybe you're only able to commit to creating one video per week. As a comparison, Dr. Berg, who is a highly successful client of mine, created daily videos for years, but if that isn't realistic to you right now, it's okay. The idea here is to commit to the journey itself.

Commitment is the foundation of any successful journey. Without it, we fall off the path and lose sight of our goals. So, figure out what you can do now and commit to *that*.

Step Two: Improve the quality of your message.

When you first start on this content journey, you may find yourself worrying about the quality of your message or the media (video, audio, visuals) used to deliver that message.

Here's a friendly reminder: We all start somewhere, and starting raw and imperfect is okay. In fact, it may even be more relatable to the audiences you first start to reach.

Now, it goes without saying that quality should always be something to strive for. The better your message and the more engaging it is, the more likely it will reach and impinge upon people. But this is something that doesn't need to be perfected from day one. Through practice and experience, the quality of your content will naturally improve.

With that said, working on the quality of your *message* should be a priority over the technical improvements. What makes a quality message? One that is easy to understand and benefits the viewer in some way. Of course, there are many factors that can go into great content, but here are a few tips you can start with:

1. Answer questions that are being asked related to your niche. You can find this out by searching relevant terms on each platform, or you can use sites like www.answerthepublic.com. Use this to inspire your content.
2. Make sure the content is a complete communication. You can do this by creating an outline before you start. To avoid leaving your audience hanging, ensure that it has a clear beginning and end.
3. Focus on providing value in the form of entertainment, inspiration, or education. Value is what transforms you from a stranger in the eyes of your viewers into someone they can trust.

Remember, attention is earned, not given. You do so by offering value that the viewer can use immediately, which in turn improves some aspect of their lives. You don't need to solve all their problems in one video, but you should offer enough value to spark an improvement. This concept is universal and applies to all types of businesses: from taxes and health to real estate and software development. Regardless of the industry, always make it a priority to deliver value in every piece of content you create.

Understanding the art of creating quality content is just the beginning. As we continue to hone this skill, it's equally important to amplify our efforts. Let's dive into the next step: ramping up our quantity of content to widen our reach and impact.

Step Three: Increase the quantity of your content.

In today's busy online landscape, capturing *attention* must be your primary goal, and quantity of content plays a significant role in accomplishing just that. This applies even more when you're just getting started.

If you look at some of the top content creators, you'll notice that many of them post multiple times a day. Gary Vaynerchuk, as an example, posts approximately 3+ times/day, but a good goal to start with is at least once per day, ideally on each of the platforms you are posting on.

If you're feeling a bit overwhelmed by the idea of posting daily on multiple platforms, don't worry. I'll be sharing more about how to make the entire process easier and more efficient in the next chapter. But for now, your goal is simple: Make more content.

Finally, as a bit of encouragement, the more you do this, the easier this process will become. You'll find better and faster ways of coming up with ideas and recording content.

Once again, in the world of social media and business, attention is currency, and the more you can get, the greater your success will be. Therefore, the more content you can create and post, the more "omnipresent" you'll be, which ultimately translates into faster success and more revenue.

To recap, getting your content creation journey off the ground involves:

Step One: Making a commitment to the journey.

Step Two: Improving the quality of your message.

Step Three: Increasing the quantity of your content.

Even after his passing, my father's content continues to have a huge impact on the continued growth of our NaturalSlim® brand. Although no new content has been created for several years now, we continue to rinse and repeat what I mentioned in Step Three above by repurposing the thousands of videos that were recorded before he passed. This allows us to keep capturing an ever-growing amount of attention.

This is just the beginning of an exciting journey towards creating a legacy for yourself and your brand. You never know how far your words, images or videos will reach, or how long they'll continue to make an impact, but as long as you apply what I covered here, you'll be headed in the right direction.

HOW TO BE EVERYWHERE

"When I hear people say, 'You're everywhere!' I know I'm doing it right."
The Ninja Says

Success in the game of business is dictated by one thing: attention. The more you can get, the easier it will be for you to expand. When it comes to creating content for social media, the best way to accomplish this is by being omnipresent. In other words, you want to be everywhere.

Although there are a few giants among social media platforms, users typically spend most of their time on just one or a couple of them. While some may prefer scrolling through their Facebook feed or exploring YouTube, others may exclusively live on TikTok or Instagram.

To top it off, each of these platforms often has a variety of "placements," which are sections of a platform where a particular type of content exists. Each of these placements and types of content is consumed differently.

For example, as of the time of this writing (2023), Instagram has three major placements:

- Feed Posts, where you'll find a combination of video and image posts.
- Reels, where you'll find only vertical videos.

- Stories, where you'll find images and videos that disappear after 24 hours.

As a side note, this was wildly different only 5 years ago when "Reels" didn't exist yet, and long-form vertical videos could be found under a different placement called IGTV. Today, IGTV is gone, and Reels are the only form of video on Instagram. Interesting how things change, isn't it?

The reality is, your potential audience could be primarily on any one of these platforms, actively consuming one or two of the placements within it. Reels, for example, are a very popular form of content today, and many Instagram users spend hours on just that one placement alone. On the other hand, some of your potential audience may be "living" mostly on YouTube, where they watch longer, in-depth videos about the subjects they are interested in.

If you were to post on only one platform, there's a good chance you're not reaching a very large percentage of your potential audience. This is why it's important to be omnipresent.

So, does this mean you need to become a full-time content creator and dump all your other responsibilities? Not at all.

The trick is to create content that works for as many platforms as possible. Luckily, each of these platforms have enough common denominators that you can create a few types of content that works for all of them. As of this writing, these types of content are:

- Long-form landscape videos
- Short-form vertical videos
- Images
- Text

It might feel a little daunting trying to figure out how you're going to create a bunch of content in all these formats. The good news is that there is an easier way to go about it, and it's something that we do for many of our branding clients at my marketing agency. Let me give you an example of how this works.

Let's say we start with a 10-minute, detailed video about a specific subject, perhaps "The First Step to Success: Finding Your Superpower." At my agency, we refer to this video as "Primary Content," because it becomes the primary source of all other types of content such as short clips, text (quotes, blogs, etc.), audio (for podcasts), etc. Here's a visual of what this breakdown looks like:

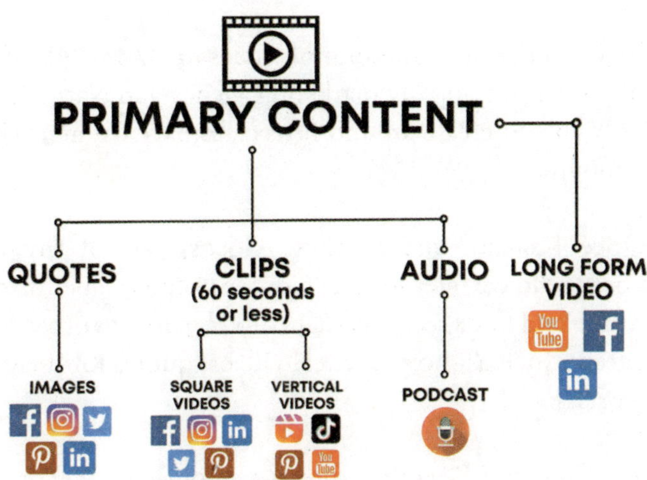

So, from this 10-minute video, we could theoretically create the following:

- A complete YouTube video
- Multiple quote cards (images with impactful quotes)

- Multiple short clips from sections of the video that work well on their own
- Multiple text posts
- A blog/article (sometimes more than one)
- A podcast (also, sometimes more than one)

The quantity of each will vary depending on the length of the Primary Content and what is covered, but with this process, you're able to turn a single piece of content into several that can then be used across multiple social media platforms.

As a real example, I share thousands of posts monthly across a variety of social media platforms for my own personal brand, most of which revolve around the subjects of marketing and business.

Now, do I create thousands of videos to do this? Absolutely not! Between running my marketing agency and NaturalSlim®, I'm only able to create around fifteen Primary Content videos every month.

Once I create one of these videos, one of my team members, who we refer to as a "Content Miner," goes through that video and finds sections that could be used as other forms of content, such as short, vertical videos, quotes for images or text posts, etc.

The Content Miner then directs a graphic designer or video editor to create the graphics or videos. In this way, we could potentially turn a single 10-minute video into:

- Three to five 15-60 second vertical clips
- One podcast (extracted audio)
- Eight to ten quote cards (pulled from the content)
- Eight to ten text-only posts

- One or two blogs (a thousand words per blog)

This is how you become omnipresent and with it, you can reach a larger potential audience. This system has helped build successful brands like Dr. Eric Berg and Frank Suarez and continues to promote growth at extraordinary speeds for other brands I work with.

Personally, when I hear people say, "Manuel, you're everywhere. You're a content machine," I know I'm doing it right. If I don't hear that enough, I need to amplify my message. Remember, attention equals revenue, so the more you can get, the better.

If you want to dive into this subject a bit more, scan the QR code below to get access to my Social Media Omnipresence Execution Training link:

A common concern about posting a lot of content is the possibility of annoying your followers. There are two things to consider here. First, your ideal audience who needs and/or wants the information you're sharing will stick around. In other words, your content will act as a filter, only leaving those who are your ideal audience. Second, not every piece of content you make will be seen by every one of your followers every time you post.

With today's social media algorithms, your followers are not only seeing posts from several other people they follow (could be hundreds!), but also content from "suggested accounts". In other words, your content is likely just another needle in a haystack, making this yet another reason to post more.

If you're worried about people unfollowing you, just know this: it's a part of the game. I've had plenty of friends, family and students unfollow me many times over. It's something you have to try not to take personally. But you know what keeps me going? My belief in my message and using it to help others, which leads me to my next point.

Creating and posting large amounts of content solely for the purpose of selling your products or service will not only be a waste of your time, but it won't help you in the long run. As long as you focus on genuinely helping others with your knowledge and experience, posting frequently will only bring you closer to your goals faster.

Probably the most powerful result of following this strategy is that it can help you avoid wasting a ton of money on advertising. Creating an online presence is the best introduction you and your brand can have with the world at large. It's the "icebreaker" of the digital world and works far better than running ads to an audience who has no idea who you are, but more on that in a later chapter.

Ready to learn how to add some fuel to the fire to make this process faster? Let's explore that in the next chapter.

INVESTING IN ATTENTION

"Investing in attention isn't necessary to win,
but it can make the entire process much faster."
The Ninja Says

In my marketing training, I stress the importance of leveraging advertising to boost your impact and bring more attention to your message. Although it's not necessary, promoting your value-based content on social media can speed up the process. Remember, your number one goal is to capture attention.

If you're like me, eager to conquer the world by capitalizing on today's opportunities and you have some extra funds to invest, then it's worth putting it behind your value-based content.

I will admit, there was a point where I advised against "boosting" your content. But this was only because the targeting options were very limited. Today, it's a different story, and "boosting" can actually be a very effective tool for anyone looking to expedite the process of building brand awareness.

The reality is, making a sale at the first contact is unlikely for most, but even a small daily investment of $2 to $5 can reap great rewards in the long run. One of the great things about this digital era is that you can advertise without long-term commitments, unlike traditional marketing, such as magazines, radio, or TV. With minimal investment, you can reach a large audience on social media platforms for the cost of a daily cup of coffee.

As of 2023, for example, less than five dollars on Facebook could put your message in front of a thousand potential customers. Then, when your content begins to generate interest, social media algorithms will help drive even more traffic your way, creating a beautiful cycle where one element fuels the next.

Today's leading social media platforms are massive with billions of monthly active users. No other companies provide the potential to reach such a huge audience. Not to mention, every potential customer or client is likely on these platforms every single day. But this also means that there is an enormous number of businesses and brands also trying to capture some of that attention.

Every one of these platforms profits from this attention, making their platforms even more valuable to those who want to leverage it to grow their businesses. Year after year, as these platforms continue to grow, organic reach has gradually declined, making it harder to rely entirely on ad-free marketing.

For example, you may only reach around five percent of your Facebook followers with your content organically. If you have 100,000 followers, only 5,000 or less might see your content. If you want to extend your reach, advertising is your answer. It amplifies your reach, resulting in growth of audiences, followers, engagement, and overall visibility.

So, how do we begin investing in getting our content seen? How do we know which content to put money behind? How much should you spend? How do we tell if our money is being well spent or not?

First, you need to start by creating and posting your content consistently for at least a week. During this week, you need to see which of your posts people are really loving. On every social platform, you'll have access to some form of analytics, which is what you'll be using to see how your content is performing.

The two key metrics you need to keep an eye on are "reach" and "engagement". As a note, these terms may vary a bit from platform to platform. Reach is super important, as it represents how far the algorithm is pushing it out. In other words, the larger the reach, the more people that are seeing it.

So, a post with a lot of reach might be a good one to promote, even if people aren't interacting with it much. That might seem weird, but again, high reach tells us that the platform is showing your content to a lot of people, which we want.

Now, let's talk about engagement. This metric will tell you which of your posts people are interacting with the most in the form of comments, likes and/or shares. It is also a good way to determine which of your posts to promote.

When you see that there's a particular piece of content that is performing well in terms of reach and engagement, then you can add a little fuel to the fire. The amount you spend is entirely up to you, your goals and ultimately, what you can afford. Whether that's $5/day or $500/day, this is a personal choice you need to make on what you can personally afford and how quickly you want to get your content seen by a larger audience.

Speaking of audiences, an important subject to become familiar with is audience targeting. I've seen it time and time again where even the "best" content shown in front of the wrong audience will not produce results, but sub-par or even low quality content shown to the right audience can perform really well.

So it's worth the time to figure out who exactly is your audience. You can target your content to people based on their interests, where they live, their age, etc. Figuring this out will be key to your success with any paid advertising you do.

Need more help with audience targeting? Scan the QR code below to get my latest resource on this topic:

Remember that using ads to "boost" your content isn't necessarily something you have to do. It's entirely possible to grow your audience without investing any money at all, as long as you're regularly sharing content that your audience finds valuable in some way. The difference is how quickly you'll see growth.

No matter which way you choose to go, the most important thing is to stay focused on your goals. Keep learning, keep growing, and over time, you'll see that your influence will gradually start to expand.

Now, onto the last and most exciting step of this formula: turning that attention into revenue!

TURNING ATTENTION INTO REVENUE

"The money is in what you do with the list."
The Ninja Says

What I'll be sharing in this chapter is vital. One of the biggest misconceptions I've noticed over the years in the world of social media is the assumption that a massive following across all platforms somehow equals success. If you look at this closely, you'll notice a large number of influencers, despite how many "followers" or "subscribers" they might have, aren't financially secure. The reality is that most of them are struggling.

Getting attention is one thing but turning that attention into revenue is another ball game entirely. On the other hand, without attention, no revenue can be generated. So, to be successful, think of this journey as an engine. All the parts need to work together in harmony for the whole system to function effectively.

To break it down further, there are five key categories or "pillars" that are essential for successfully marketing your business and brand:

1. Content (the message)
2. Marketing (the distribution)
3. Lead Generation (funneling audiences into the brand's lists)

4. Sales (self-explanatory)
5. Nurture (encouraging people to make a purchase, and to continue doing so in the future).

Each of these pillars is crucial and holds significant power on its own.

In this chapter, we will dive into the third pillar: Lead Generation. The reality is that businesses are in danger without "identities" (phone numbers, emails, physical addresses). While *content* represents your message and the value you provide to audiences, *marketing* is how you disseminate your content (or value) by leveraging available opportunities to achieve the most attention at the least possible cost.

So, let's say you've successfully generated some attention. First, well done! You're already ahead of most of your competitors. Now it's time to convert that attention into revenue, and the best way to do this is by funneling those people into your own lists and marketing channels, such as SMS (text messages), Email Service Providers (ESP), and

Customer Relationship Management (CRM) software. This is the foundation on which sustainable businesses are built.

But why is this important? First, having your own list puts you in control of your own marketing. Some social platforms have certain restrictions on what you can or cannot say or advertise. The supplement world is particularly affected by this. So, by having your own list, you can overcome many of these restrictions.

Second, something to consider is that although these massive social platforms can play a huge part in your success by giving you access to their giant network of users, they can also pull the plug on you whenever they want. Although this doesn't necessarily happen often, it can and has happened, and when it does, there goes your attention. Thus, building a list not only puts you in control of your own marketing, but protects you from losing your entire audience overnight.

So, you grow your list. Then what? There's an old marketing adage that goes, "The money is in the list." However, I think this is better worded as, "The money is in what you *do* with the list."

Before I get into the details of what you can do with that list, let me paint the whole picture: The first step is creating content that puts your Superpower, your message in front of the right people. Then, you get that content posted everywhere, and maybe you invest some money to push it out even further. As you do this, you'll be building your social media audience. The focus here is providing value, value, value.

Once you have an audience on social media, then you can start building your list through lead generation strategies. The possibilities for this are virtually limitless, especially when you have valuable information in your business that potential customers can use to improve some aspect of their lives.

Here are some of the main strategies that have helped me generate over five million "identities" for the brands I manage and own over the past few years:

1. Organize a contest or challenge where participants can win your products or services. These contests or challenges can be anything from sharing your content, recording a creative video that somehow relates to your brand/product/service, etc.
2. Create mini-courses that provide knowledge within your area of expertise. These mini-courses can be in the form of a video, text or even a series of emails.
3. Create valuable, high-quality eBooks or PDFs that address a specific problem relevant to your business, products and/or services.
4. Offer exclusive, early access to new products, sales, or services for those who sign up to your newsletter.
5. Create an engaging quiz relevant to your industry and provide value-packed results that help them with some specific problem.

Again, with each of these, the focus must be on providing value. By doing this, you not only build trust, but you position yourself or your brand as an expert in your industry.

As a note, lead generation strategies are typically free for those opting in. The only "exchange" is their contact information (such as a phone number and/or email). Where you ask for this information may vary depending on the strategy.

For example, for a free PDF that covers a specific problem they need help with, you'd likely want to ask for that information first. However, in a quiz, you might want to wait until you reach the end of the quiz and then ask for that information in exchange for the results.

Now, once you generate a lead, the focus shifts to nurturing them, converting them into paying customers, and maintaining a relationship with them to encourage repeat purchases. Here are a few ways you can do this:

- **Email Marketing:** Send personalized emails such as informative updates, tips related to your product/service, additional free resources related to their interests, exciting sales, engaging surveys, captivating stories, and more.
- **Webinars/Seminars**: Host regular webinars or seminars that provide further value and demonstrate your expertise. These can be free or paid, depending on the value and depth of information provided.
- **Customer Loyalty Programs:** Develop a loyalty program that rewards repeat customers. This not only encourages further purchases, but it also helps build a strong, loyal customer base.
- **Social Media Engagement:** Continue to engage with your audience on social media. Encourage them to interact with your posts and respond to their comments and messages.

Again, the focus here should be primarily on providing value!

A common question I get is how often you should communicate with them? Is there such a thing as too much? In my marketing company, I operate under this principle: "Block or Buy." If you believe in your message and know that your products and services will improve someone's life, then you should persist until they either buy what you're selling or opt-out.

And when someone opts out of your communications, this doesn't mean it's the end of your journey. It simply means these people aren't ready to buy just yet. What you can do with these people is funnel them back into your social platforms, such as Facebook, and retarget them with your value-based content, excluding those who are very clearly not interested in your message, of course.

Remember, the overall goal of lead generation and nurturing is to convert prospects into paying customers and then maintain a strong relationship with them. It's not just about making a one-time sale; it's about building a long-term relationship with them.

As we come to the end of covering the various steps of the Primary Strategy, let's review all the steps again:

1. Find out what your Superpower is.
2. Start creating valuable content to share your knowledge and message with the world. Focus on helping others.
3. Use existing channels to share your content.
4. Commit to creating and posting content consistently.
5. Ramp up your efforts by creating and posting even more content on as many platforms as possible.
6. Add fuel to the fire by investing in ads that push your successful content out even further.
7. Start building your list through lead generation strategies.
8. Present your product/service only to those who have benefited from your Superpower via your content.

Again, this is a strategy that has helped me successfully build multiple brands to heights I never imagined. Now it's your turn to apply these same steps to your own journey.

THE MAKING OF A LEGACY

The Inspiring Journey Behind MetabolismoTV®

This book, as you know, is dedicated in a big way to my dad. Besides being my hero, he was one of the best Content Unicorns I have ever known. In fact, a big part of the Primary Strategy was inspired by him. Through his passion for a single subject, he was not only able to help thousands of people, but his content became a powerful source of fuel for his own brand, NaturalSlim®.

Even several years after his passing, his content reaches thousands of new people every single day and continues to bring NaturalSlim® to new heights every year.

Between MetabolismoTV® and the various social channels that are all based on my dad's content, we created the ideal marketing scenario where our customers come to us ready to buy.

Within these next few pages, I'm going to share a little about the story behind MetabolismoTV® and how it not only became one of the top health-related YouTube Channels in the world, but the game-changing factor that turned my father and his brand, NaturalSlim®, into a true legacy.

To help tell this story, I'm going to have Jorge Torres, my father's Creative Director who worked closely with him since 2006, share some parts of the journey from his perspective.

Jorge was the man behind the camera in all 2,450+ episodes that were created. Without him, we wouldn't be where we are today.

Q: When did you start working with my dad?

I started sometime in 2006, which was around the same year that Frank wrote "The Power of Your Metabolism" in Spanish. My first job was to create commercials for NaturalSlim®, but this eventually evolved into creating content for social media.

Q: How did MetabolismoTV® get started?

It wasn't until 2010 that we started working on MetabolismoTV®, but before that, the entire idea was inspired by Gary Vaynerchuk's book, "Crush It", where he talks about creating his own channel called, "Wine Library TV". In that book, there was a chapter titled "Building My Brand", and on one of the pages, he literally wrote "MetabolismoTV.com" along the margin. That was the beginning of it all.

The YouTube channel still hadn't been created yet because we were worried that people would steal our content. So, instead, we created our own channel on our website, www.MetabolismoTV.com. We generated our own traffic by creating commercials for it. This got us about 3,000 views per week, which is pretty different from the thousands of views we get every minute today.

Q: When did MetabolismoTV® start to take off?

It wasn't until Frank was finally convinced to put everything on YouTube that things started to explode. By that point, we already had 200 episodes that we had created for the private platform. For a few weeks, we uploaded a few every day to YouTube.

Q: Why do you think Frank was as successful as he was?

First, Frank was passionate about the topic. For most of his life, he personally struggled with being overweight. So, he tried a bunch of different diets and methods, and in the process of learning everything he could, he managed to figure it out and lose weight.

Naturally, people started to notice and asked him how he did it, which is what inspired him to write his book, "The Power of Your Metabolism." In total, he had about a decade of experience on this subject before even starting his brand, NaturalSlim®.

One thing he wasn't motivated by was money. I believe that if your focus is money-related, you'll end up compromising the value of your content. Frank took everything he knew about the metabolism and put it all into his book and his content. He didn't hold any of it back. Even when mentioning NaturalSlim® supplements, he'd tell the reader or viewer how to find them themselves at a local grocery store, and even how to take it.

Q: You mentioned that Gary Vaynerchuk was a big inspiration behind MetabolismoTV®. What do you think was Frank's biggest takeaway from Gary's advice?

Frank highlighted one part in his copy of "Crush It" where Gary said, "Money follows the eyeballs", and I could tell that Frank applied this concept the entire time. His motivation was always to help others, and that alone captured attention. Do you know how many people were able to successfully lose weight just by reading his book or watching his videos? Thousands.

So, now you have thousands of people who trust Frank Suarez and MetabolismoTV®, sharing their successes online for others to see. Then, you have those that discover along the way that they have a "slow metabolism". So, who do you think these people are going to go to when they realize they need some help? NaturalSlim®, of course.

Even almost a decade later, those same episodes from so long ago are still helping people. Those who weren't overweight then, are now struggling, come across those videos, apply what Frank taught, and start the cycle all over again.

Q: Based on your experience in working so closely with a Content Unicorn, what advice would you give to someone who wants to start creating content?

First, you have to be passionate about your topic. If you're not, this isn't the way to go. Not to mention, people can tell if you're genuinely passionate or not. If you're creating content and all you're seeing are dollar signs, it will hinder your growth. People will see right through that.

Next, your purpose has to be rooted in helping others and you need to be willing to give it all away for free. By doing this, you're planting a seed that will eventually grow into a tree that you can eat from.

Q: When is the best time to start creating content?

As a foundation, you need to have the experience, purpose, and passion for the topic you're wanting to create content on. Then, see if you can create a list of at least 50 topics that you could talk about. If you can do that, it's a good time to start.

Q: What's the best way to keep creating content?

Stay on top of what is trending and what people are saying in the comments. Most of the content that Frank created later on was based on the comments that people left. This turns your content into a conversation with your audience and allows you to create variations of content based on their perspective of the subjects you cover. This is how we created over 2000 episodes and kept them feeling fresh.

Q: What kind of planning needs to go into creating content?

Before we recorded anything, Frank would spend at least thirty to forty-five minutes outside of the studio, planning what he was going to cover in each episode. Then, before we'd start recording an episode, I'd ask him a few questions about it to narrow down how he was going to cover the topic. I'd play the part of the audience and ask questions that I thought they would have, so that the end result would be easy for people to absorb.

Doing this really helped with the overall outcome of the content. One thing that people really liked about Frank's content was how he could turn a complicated subject into something that could be easily understood.

Q: What should every piece of content include?

First, every piece of content should provide some kind of value. You want the viewer to feel empowered by the knowledge you gave them.

Second, you need to make sure that every piece of content is complete. In other words, everything that the viewer would need to know to solve a specific problem would be included in that one video. You don't want to make them watch five different videos to get the whole idea.

Q: What do you think is more important? Quantity or quality?

Neither. Consistency is more important than both. Everyone will have different amounts of time to devote to creating content. If that means you can only produce two videos per week, that's okay.

Once you have the consistency figured out, you'll want to focus on quality. And by "quality", I'm not talking about the camera, lights, microphone, etc. It's the quality of your message, including the information you are sharing. Of course, all these various technical elements are important, but they are secondary to your message and value.

After that comes quantity. When you have consistent content going out and the quality of your content has proven to be successful, you can increase your quantity.

Q: How do I measure my success?

All our efforts with MetabolismoTV® directly affected NaturalSlim®. If the content performed well, we saw an increase in sales. Views and followers are definitely a metric, but they are not your bottom line. Ultimately, if the content produced more sales, we knew it was quality content.

My dad's story is a clear example of what passion, purpose, and a genuine care for others can achieve. His dedication turned MetabolismoTV® into an ever-growing legacy.

The takeaways are simple: Be genuine, know what you're talking about, and most importantly, aim to help. Don't worry about fancy equipment – it's your message that counts.

Start now, with whatever you have. Build a connection with your audience, stay consistent, and let your passion be the driving force.

This is how you create a legacy that will last through generations. Now it's your turn to create your own. What are you waiting for?

THE MIND OF A NINJA

"You can either give up, or push harder, and only one of those will bring you closer to your goals."
The Ninja Says

In the next few chapters, I'm going to share some of the mental aspects of my journey that I feel played a part in getting me to where I am today. To be honest, I don't spend a lot of time thinking about my mindset, but after looking back at everything I've gone through personally, I feel like there may be a few things I can pass along to you that could help you through your own journey towards your goals.

"The Millionaire Mindset"

Now that I've reached the "millionaire" status financially, it's interesting to look back at where I started mindset-wise. As you've probably gathered by now, I didn't start off with a "millionaire mindset." In fact, I had very little confidence in my own abilities, so the idea of reaching the level of financial freedom I now have was very unreal for a long time. What turned this around for me was the need to provide a better life for myself and my family.

Today, I don't have financial limitations like I once did. I have the freedom to donate generously, help my family and employees, and even indulge in practically anything I want.

It still feels unreal when I go shopping and realize I can buy anything I want, considering this was so different just over a decade ago.

I'm not telling you this to brag, but to paint a picture. This lifestyle I've earned for myself, again, is something I only dreamed of in the past.

Looking back, this particular mindset seemed to form naturally over time, but I believe there are a few aspects of it that you can start to work on now to help you get there.

First, you need to find your passion. What are you passionate about? What drives you? What could you spend endless amounts of time on and never get tired of? For me, it's not just about the money, but the impact I can make and the number of lives I can improve.

I also truly love what I do. I'm excited to wake up and work with my team. I consider them an extension of my family who are working by my side to conquer goals together.

When you love what you do, there is no such thing as "working too hard." Work only becomes unbearable when you're doing something you don't like. You'll find yourself counting the minutes until the clock hits 5:00 pm. It's really a terrible way to live.

If you don't have a passion yet, start looking. Try different things if you need to. Your passion will be the foundation of everything you do, and it's the one thing that will get you through the thick and thin of your journey.

Another factor that I feel contributed to this "millionaire mindset" is confidence. Like I mentioned earlier, I didn't start my journey as confident as I am now. I was full of doubts, but the one thing that helped me overcome it was execution. In other words, I would push my doubts aside and do whatever was necessary to get results. With every "win", my confidence would grow, until one day, I truly believed in myself. But the way to get past doubts and worry is to just DO and continue *doing* until you start to get results. Over time, you'll find that your uncertainties will begin to fade away and, in their place, you'll start becoming more confident.

Overcoming Pessimism

Pessimism is a tricky mindset to be in, as it will literally stop you from achieving much of anything. The good news is that there is a way out.

First, you have to put yourself in the right environment. This includes the people you are around. Being around pessimistic people will only breed more negativity and ultimately hold you down. These are the types of people that will make you doubt yourself, and sometimes, they can be the closest ones to you. Even worse, they can sometimes be hard to spot because their advice is "for your own good" or delivered in such a way that seems reasonable. Maybe they're constantly telling you to "take it easy" or to slow down and enjoy life. Who knows.

It's not that anyone who tells you these types of things is bad, necessarily. They may just not fully understand what makes *you* happy in life, or maybe they're genuinely concerned about your health and well-being. Regardless, you must be true to your own goals, and if that means not being around these types of people for a while, then do that.

Just like some diseases, pessimism is contagious. Luckily, optimism is also contagious. So, put yourself around the right people that will help put you in the mindset you need to accomplish your goals.

Now, maybe there isn't anyone stopping you but yourself. This can come in the form of negative self-talk, self-doubt, laziness, etc.

First, you're doing the correct thing by learning more and connecting with people that are like-minded. Reading books, taking courses, and attending conferences are ways you can break out of this habit of bringing yourself down.

That›s the key to success. If you look closely at every single successful individual, you'll find that they decided to make themselves better and dedicate themselves to getting educated.

The way to break through stopping yourself is by learning more and putting yourself around the right people. That's how you are going to break through any barriers that you're putting up for yourself.

Setting Goals

I've seen all types of methods of goal setting, from writing them down every morning to saying them to yourself in a mirror. Regardless of the method, I do believe that being clear about your goals is important, but how you do it is up to you.

I'll share what I currently do to give you some inspiration. At the end of every year, I write down what I intend to accomplish for the next year, including personal and professional goals. Since my family is at the center of all of it and involved in all aspects of my life, I also include their goals in this. Where my wife and I have our own professional goals, my kids have academic goals.

This is something I've been doing since 2014, and it has been very interesting to look back at what I wrote back then. In fact, one of the first big goals I had was to generate one hundred thousand in revenue every month. Fast forward to today, and that figure, on average, is over seven hundred thousand every month.

On a day-to-day basis, I don't write my long-term goals down, but I do make it a point to write down everything I'd like to accomplish that day. This is something I insist that all my team members do, as it helps tremendously with how much we're all able to accomplish each day.

So, find a system that works for you. Whichever way you choose to set your goals, your first step should be to clarify them so you know exactly what you're working towards. Be as specific as possible. The main thing is to keep this goal at the top of your mind so that the majority of your day-to-day, or week-to-week actions contribute to getting closer to that goal.

Staying Motivated

I don't personally use positive affirmations or mantras to keep myself motivated, but I do believe in the power of the will of an individual.

What motivates each of us will vary from person to person, but for me, I'm not necessarily motivated by just building the tallest building in the city. I'm more interested in helping others also build their own buildings alongside mine. This includes students who want to learn from me, those watching my content online, and even my team.

Besides that, I consider myself somewhat of a fearless competitor. I have very high expectations of myself, and if I'm being totally honest, I'm very bothered by failures.

With that said, when I do experience a loss, I use it as motivation to improve myself, learn more, and get back to work. Any game, including the game of business, will inevitably be full of losses, but it's persistence and push-through that will get you to those major wins.

Over the years I've had my fair share of doors closed in my face. Instead of feeling sorry for myself, I turn that energy towards doing everything I can to prove that they made a mistake. To be clear, this isn't something I do out of hate or resentment, but simply out of a desire to succeed.

So, my best advice here is this: Work on your goals every day and keep your eye on the prize. Focus on getting that first win, second win, and so on. When losses happen (and they will), use them as motivation to keep learning more and pushing harder. Experiences are all about how you respond to them. You can either give up, or push harder, and only one of those will bring you closer to your goals.

Embracing the Journey

Any goal worth achieving will take some time and effort to make it a reality. You'll go through your fair share of obstacles and moments where it all feels impossible. You'll likely even doubt your ability to make it through. But one day, you'll start to see a light at the end of the tunnel. You'll get that little bit of hope you needed to confirm that what you're working towards isn't just a dream, but something real and attainable.

Then, before you know it, you'll find yourself sitting in the life you've been working so hard for. But what now? Is this the finish line? Do you sit back and say, "I've made it"?

Here's what I think – the real magic is in the journey, not the destination. When you're doing what you love every day, *that* is the real victory.

So, the goal, as I see it, is to find something you love to do so much that it doesn't feel like work. I truly believe that everyone can find this.

For those of you reading this, your mission is to find that one thing you'd happily do for the rest of your life. Don't know where to start? Learn more. Do more. Try as many things as you can.

And when you do find it, hold on tight. Let it be the fuel that gets you out of bed every morning. As I see it, a goal is just the beginning of an adventure, and the adventure is where you'll be spending most of your time. Might as well enjoy it, right?

My hope for you is that when all is said and done, you'll be able to look back and say, "I loved every minute of it."

ACHIEVING SUCCESS OUTSIDE THE SYSTEM

"The larger your dreams and goals are, the stronger your hunger for knowledge needs to be."
The Ninja Says

Despite not having a degree from a prestigious university or a flawless academic record, my passion for learning has fueled my journey. The truth is that even top-performing students who graduate with honors often find themselves struggling in life. I've even met a few myself. So, let my journey be proof to you that no matter how well (or not) you did in school, you can still accomplish great things.

If you look closely, you'll find that most successful entrepreneurs have a systematic approach to self-improvement and a never-ending thirst for knowledge. To them, there isn't a "cap" when it comes to education. They just keep learning, no matter how successful they become.

A metaphor that I like to use to demonstrate the mind's potential is this: While a trashcan will eventually overflow when filled beyond its limit, the mind is limitless. With that said, it's important to be aware of what you're dumping into it, because you want to avoid filling it up with trash that will slow or damage your progress.

Regardless of how much I grow, my learning journey never ends. I prefer listening to educational podcasts over listening to music, watching TV, reading novels, or playing video games. I believe that your drive to learn should directly correspond to the size of your dreams and goals. If you're a long way from where you'd like to be, strive to learn something new every day. On the other hand, if you're satisfied with how life is going right now, feel free to indulge in leisure activities. But my guess is that isn't the case if you're reading this book. So, the larger your dreams and goals are, the stronger your hunger for knowledge needs to be.

The desire to keep learning is what got me to where I am today, but that wasn't always the case. Before becoming an entrepreneur, I would often waste a lot of time. I was a nine-to-five employee, and learning simply wasn't something I was interested in. I would leave work and spend hours watching television or playing games on my phone.

That went on for some time until I realized my own potential for growth. Over time, as I began seeing results, I became obsessed with not only learning, but with getting even more results. I began to believe in myself and my own abilities. From that point on, I made it my responsibility to live a life not only for myself, but for future generations.

Time has become my greatest and most valuable commodity. It's not that my life is "all work and no play". That couldn't be further from the truth because I love what I do career-wise, but when it comes to leisure activities, I'm very picky about what I spend my time on. For example, I'll spend a few hours watching my favorite football team play or watching an incredible movie with zero regrets. But if I find myself doing something that I don't really enjoy, it's a waste of time.

So, it's important to spend your time in a way that matches your goals. If what you're doing doesn't help you reach your dreams, you should reevaluate what you're doing. Your goals and your actions need to align.

Learning can be a barrier for some. Take marketing, for example. There's a lot to know between the various platforms, how to create an ad, how to target the right audience, and so on. Luckily, we live in an era where access to information and knowledge is truly unlimited. All you need to do is look for it. I also know that the amount of information available can sometimes be overwhelming. There's a lot of it and some of it may even conflict. So, how do you choose the right one?

Personally, this is what I do to get past this. First, I look for mentors who have already accomplished the goals I'm working towards. There's no real reason for me to spend time listening to someone who hasn't achieved that yet. Of course, there are a handful of people who like to "fake-it-til-you-make-it" and may post photos with a rented luxury car or borrowed yacht. This is a big reason why I look for evidence of their success before I spend my time learning from them.

At the beginning of my journey, every spare minute I had was spent learning how to build a private-label brand on Amazon. The course I was taking was by one of my first teachers, Jason Fladlien, who I consider to be one of the greatest marketers alive. Through Jason's training and webinars, I discovered yet another brilliant marketer, Ben Cummings, who is a big part of why I stepped into the marketing world professionally. In fact, my first time on stage was in 2017, where I spoke to his audience about Facebook marketing.

Between Jason and Ben, both of which were accomplishing great things (and still are today), I learned everything I could about what they had to teach.

Over the years I've made a rule for myself to learn from no more than two mentors at a time. Any more than that makes it hard for me to effectively absorb and apply what they're teaching. The mentors I learn from have changed over the years, but I always limit myself to learning from no more than two at a time.

Today, I'm still learning from Jason Fladlien, who has become a client of mine. He's on social media now and for the first time, we're growing his channels, including his podcast, which I listen to every day on my way to and from work.

Gary Vaynerchuk is another mentor I listen to today that I've had since the beginning of my journey. In fact, he's the one that influenced the content strategy that turned NaturalSlim® into a major success story. We even had the opportunity to sit down with him at one point to map out the next steps for NaturalSlim®, which was an experience in and of itself.

So, start looking for mentors with a proven track record, and feel free to use my same rule of learning from no more than two at any given time. From my experience, doing it this way helps me avoid getting overwhelmed by the huge amount of information out there. This allows me to learn a specific method, try it out exactly as the mentor suggests, and discover for myself if it is usable. This is like taking dieting advice. You will never know what works unless you apply one method long enough to find out.

Finally, a vital part of this process is time management. Look at your daily routine and find anything you're doing that isn't contributing to your development or success. You might be surprised by how much time you can free up by eliminating these distractions.

Remember, we all have the same 24 hours in a day. Even if you sleep eight hours and work another eight, that still leaves you with eight hours left. That's a lot of time.

So, start looking for mentors who have accomplished exactly what you're aiming for, absorb as much as you can from them, and most importantly, *apply* what you learn.

BECOMING A MONEY MAGNET

"Genuine care for others and big thinking is what makes people want to be a part of your journey."
The Ninja Says

Throughout my experiences so far, I've observed an interesting trait among highly successful brands and individuals: they have a unique ability to magnetize both people and money. Somehow, they can effortlessly attract attention, and thus, generate impressive revenue.

Of course, before you become a "money magnet," you have to first become a "people magnet," but how?

The first thing you need to do is create a space that makes people genuinely want to be part of your world. The secret lies in two fundamental attributes: the ability to show genuine care for others and big thinking.

Most people are naturally attracted to those who show genuine care for their well-being, as well as those who show a level of drive and professionalism that goes beyond the ordinary. It's inspiring to meet someone who wants to make the world a better place, to make a difference in people's lives, and who envisions more for themselves than most do.

My father was a great example of this, as he was more interested in hearing about how he was able to help someone recover their health than how many sales were made. He genuinely cared about people and those who watched his content could tell.

He was also a big thinker. He wanted to impact the entire world with the information he had, because he knew how many people had wrong or totally false information about the subject of weight loss and health. His passion to help others in a big way attracted millions of people and even after his passing, continues to do so.

Let's dive into how to incorporate these traits into your own life. First, you need to find your passion. If you've already determined your Superpower by now, this should be easy.

Once you have found your passion, you'll need to figure out how you can use it to help others. If you look at some of the most influential people in history, they did exactly this. They found something they were passionate about and spent their days using it to help others. In this era, doing this is easier than ever because anyone can potentially help thousands of people or more by creating and uploading a single video on one of these social media platforms.

Part of this involves listening to and interacting with those people. What do they need help with? What questions are they asking? The better you understand who they are and what they need help with, the more of an impact you'll be able to create with them.

Lastly, you'll want to work on thinking big. For some, this concept might feel challenging because many of us are content with our secure, ordinary lives. Or maybe a lack of confidence might make you feel like you can't achieve big things. I have a few suggestions on how to get around this.

First, being around the right people can make a difference here. Just like being around pessimistic people can breed pessimism, small thinking can do the same. So, find a group that thinks bigger than you do, and spend as much time as you can around them. You'll eventually find that your own mindset on this will start to change.

Second, make learning a regular part of your life. This is something I personally live by and is even incorporated into the core values of my marketing agency. Doing this will not only give you the tools you need to accomplish more but will open the door to more opportunities that may not have been visible to you prior.

Lastly, if lack of confidence or belief in yourself is an issue, focus on *doing*. Confidence is increased by doing the actions necessary to get from point A to point B, even if that means you have to close your eyes and jump in.

The more you do this, the easier all of this will become, and before you know it, thinking big will become more natural to you.

So, if you want to be a money magnet, you have to start by becoming a people magnet, which requires a never-ending drive for personal growth and a level of understanding and care that is uncommon. It involves genuinely wanting to help others. This combination of genuine care for others and big thinking is what makes people want to be a part of your journey. They see an opportunity to grow with you or to share in your success somehow, and this is what keeps them by your side.

I truly believe that this philosophy can transform your business and personal life. When you apply it, you'll find yourself achieving goals at an unimaginable pace. The power to draw people towards you, be it online or in real life, is truly magical.

JUDGING A BOOK BY ITS COVER

"People will judge you, so it's important to look and act the part you want to play."

The Ninja Says

In this chapter, I'm going to dive into the subject of judging a book by its cover, which I feel is related to the mindset you need to have to achieve big goals.

You're likely familiar with the phrase, "never judge a book by its cover." The truth is, whether we like it or not, people will associate what they see with what "success" might mean to them. It's just a fact, especially in business.

Let me paint a picture to give you a better idea. Let's say that I invited a potential marketing client to visit me in my office. The office is not only messy but also has clearly outdated equipment. I'm wearing a stained, wrinkled T-shirt, ripped jeans, and it's been a few days since I've shaved. Do you think this potential client would feel comfortable hiring me to run his marketing?

To attract business, it's essential to present yourself in a professional manner and establish a sense of trust - these two things complement each other. In other words, having a professional appearance is crucial for gaining trust. While it's not totally impossible to earn trust without looking professional, a professional appearance significantly increases your chances compared to an unprofessional one.

To be honest, there was a period of my life where I didn't act the part. I wasn't very professional in what I did, and it was very hard to get business. When I started to realize that this was affecting my ability to grow, I changed what I was doing.

Fast forward to today and everything I do and own, from my office to my website, looks very professional. I know that if I want to attract ideal clients that can pay for my premium marketing services, I have to look the part. That's just how it works.

Does this mean that you need to dip into your savings to buy an $8,000 suit or pull out a second mortgage to buy a fancy car? No. There are simple and inexpensive things you can do to accomplish the same thing, such as keeping your surroundings clean and organized, or wearing professional-looking clothes (that you can afford).

What I've noticed is that people usually feel more comfortable doing business with people comfortable investing in themselves. When you take good care of yourself, more business opportunities will come your way.

Part of this includes how you conduct business and how you interact with others. For example, if you're constantly showing up late to meetings, this will not give someone else the idea that you are a professional. However, even simple actions such as making sure your emails aren't full of typos can help with your overall image.

Looking and being a professional is a long-term plan for growing yourself, your brand, or your organization. In fact, it also applies to your social media game. The better your content looks, the more attention it will get.

With that said, don't let the need to have everything be perfect from day one stop you from getting started. Just keep this in mind as you work towards your goals and continue to grow.

In fact, I started small; my first office wasn't fancy by any means, but that didn't stop me. I just did what I could to be as professional as I could with what I had. I even created an entire digital course called Facebook Masters, which was recorded using a camera, a microphone, and a green bedsheet (as my makeshift greenscreen).

Ernesto and I in my first studio with a green bed sheet as my greenscreen.

That course made 2.5 million dollars, which I then used to grow and improve the look of my brand. In fact, just a few short years after starting Attention Grabbing Media®, we hosted the grand opening of our brand-new, state-of-the-art marketing facility. Even Nancy Cartwright, the voice of Bart Simpson, joined us!

Make it a point to work towards higher and higher levels of professionalism as you grow. People will judge you, so it's important to look and act the part you want to play. Be confident and present yourself well. When you do this, you'll have an easier time connecting with people who will help you succeed.

THE AGM® CORE VALUES

Shortly after the grand opening of the brand-new, state-of-the-art office for Attention Grabbing Media® (AGM®), I put together a series of core values for my team.

My goal with these was not only to align everyone but also to empower and inspire them to reach their full potential. They are actively applied throughout my organization, and I make it a point to have every team member focus on improving at least one of these points weekly to ensure that we grow stronger as a group.

Many of these values are based on the exact traits and mindsets I've followed to get me to where I am today. Today, they are displayed within the office, serving as a daily reminder for the whole team.

Feel free to use these as inspiration. They can help in developing your own success mindset as you work towards building the life you've always wanted. Here they are:

THE AGM® CORE VALUES:

Core Values: Traits or qualities that are not just worthwhile, but also represent an individual's or an organization's highest priorities, deeply held beliefs, and core, fundamental driving forces. They are the heart of what your organization and its employees stand for in the world. At AGM® Marketing, we — THE NINJAS — believe in the following CORE VALUES:

Be a Professional. Everything we do, we do it like a professional. We dress professionally, speak professionally, have manners, and we never tolerate sloppy work or laziness. If you are responsible for something, you give it one hundred percent, or you don't do it at all. When an action, product, or task is completed, the AGM® Ninja responsible for it should ask themselves the following question: "Are you proud of it?" The answer should invariably be "Absolutely!"

Never Stop Learning. At AGM® Marketing, we believe that the growth of our company relies entirely on individual growth, and the moment we stop learning is the exact moment we cease to grow. This same statement is applicable at an individual level. The moment you stop learning is the moment you stop earning. AGM® Ninjas are encouraged to learn daily even beyond work hours with the understanding that their growth within the group is entirely dependent on a continuous increase of their skills, which is only accomplished through a never-ending thirst and attainment of knowledge.

Positive Attitude. AGM® Marketing has ZERO TOLERANCE for negativity. An individual within the group speaking negatively about co-workers, clients or prospects will not make it within this group. We use positive language with our co-workers and clients including words and phrases like "absolutely," "definitely," "my pleasure," and "I would be happy to do that for you." An AGM® Ninja NEVER looks to explain, justify or minimize mistakes, whether real or imagined. Ninjas take responsibility for their actions and the effects they create on clients, prospects, or even coworkers. This is a very important part of our company culture.

Figure It Out (FIO). The FIO line is the oldest line in AGM®'s history. We live in an INFORMATION AGE. Whatever YOU don't know the answer to, someone else does. FIO means, "You don't know what you don't know." At AGM®, we figure things out using the massive amount of resources this internet age has to offer: Google, YouTube, articles, communities, and co-workers. Phrases like "It's not possible" or "It can't be done" have usually come to mean, "I don't have the intelligence, the energy, or the push to find an answer to this issue." An AGM® Ninja FIGURES IT OUT always, and in the process will likely discover his or her TRUE POTENTIAL.

Speed. Everything we do at AGM® Marketing, we do with speed. We follow up with speed. We send out proposals with speed. We respond to emails with speed. We answer the phones with speed. Our speed of execution brought us to where we are today and will take us to the next level. AGM® is a fast-moving rocket ship, and we consider SPEED to be one of the key ingredients to our success.

Walk the Line. AGM® Marketing is a professional company with very high expectations from clients. Every time an action, project, campaign, product, or service is completed, every AGM® Ninja involved with that project is expected to WALK THE LINE before the product is presented to a client or introduced to the world. Walking the line requires that a Ninja momentarily assumes the perspective of a client or consumer while going through the entirety of the project from start to finish to spot any imperfections, typos, malfunctions, etc. This applies to websites, chat flows, social media posts, emails, proposals, and the like.

Follow Up. At AGM® Marketing, we are responsible for getting an answer to our communications, questions, or concerns. In order to make progress, we must follow up, follow up, and follow up until we DO get an answer. We believe follow-up is one of the keys to success because it always leads to EXECUTION, which in turn leads to FORWARD PROGRESS.

Be Committed. Commitment is defined as, "The state or quality of being dedicated to a cause, activity, etc." AGM® Marketing believes that our organization will grow in direct proportion to the number of staff committed to our goals of helping small businesses flourish and prosper. Commitment requires a "MAKE IT GO RIGHT" attitude which will always lead to helping clients achieve success while working with AGM®. True AGM® Ninjas will always operate with a "WHATEVER IT TAKES" mindset when it comes to their work. At AGM®, Ninjas don't operate based on SCHEDULES — they operate based on RESULTS.

Grow Together. Every single Ninja that consistently applies the above CORE VALUES is guaranteed GROWTH as an AGM® Marketing Ninja. At AGM®, our leadership believes that a group that's winning is composed of many individuals that are also winning. AGM® leadership is committed to a culture of WEALTH SHARING, where every Ninja going above and beyond for his or her group will be able to grow as the group grows systematically.

CURRENT OPPORTUNITIES

Throughout this book, I've talked a lot about opportunities – where to find them and what to do when you come across them. In this chapter, I'd like to share a few of the current opportunities as of the writing of this book (2023).

As you know, opportunities come and go, but when you find one, it's always smart to jump on it as early as you can. For example, the first companies that decided to try to invest in AI (Artificial Intelligence) early on, such as Google and Amazon, are now top players in their industries, using AI to not only completely change how we search for things online, but also in voice recognition, such as Amazon's "Alexa."

Also, think about those who were the first to use social media platforms to advertise their businesses. Companies that saw the potential of Facebook, Instagram, and other social platforms and leveraged them before everyone else were able to build huge audiences and followings, which now gives them a big advantage in online advertising.

In these examples, those who were the first to jump on an emerging opportunity were able to use the existing momentum to achieve quite a bit of success.

It's like surfing. Just like a small wave carries the potential for a thrilling ride, being quick to recognize and act upon emerging opportunities can yield significant benefits.

So, let's jump into these current opportunities:

THE PRIVATE LABEL OPPORTUNITY

The world of the private label industry might be new to some of you, but it's more common than you might realize. Simply put, private labeling is when a company creates a product and allows other companies to purchase and rebrand it under their own name. A good example of this can be seen at your local grocery store. "Store brand" items are typically made by other manufacturers and rebranded for that specific grocery store. In other words, there may be many stores selling that exact same product, but under a different name.

Amazon is another good example of this. Many sellers offer similar or identical products such as hand sanitizers, speakers, cell phone chargers, and gardening tools, many of which are likely sourced from the same manufacturers. They use private labeling to rebrand these identical items as their own.

In fact, my business partner Ernesto and I did precisely this with our Cosy House Collection bed sheet business back in 2015, which we managed to grow into a seven-million-dollar-per-year brand with little to no initial investment.

To build a private label business without an initial investment, you'll have to find and leverage connections and opportunities. My bed sheets brand, for example, was a consignment model, so I only had to pay for the products once they sold. Over time, as sales increased, I would purchase larger quantities from China, which increased my overall profit. Six months later, we were shipping tens of thousands of bed sheets, and competing with renowned brands from my small Texas home. Not having a large investment from the start was not only helpful, but the business may not have even started if that hadn't been the case.

Now, I'm inviting you to explore the potential of private labeling in a trillion-dollar market: consumable products. These are products that are purchased repeatedly, such as supplements and skincare. Not only is it a huge opportunity to generate significant wealth, but these are the types of products that can positively impact others.

I've achieved considerable success in building supplement brands, both for myself and clients like Dr. Eric Berg and our NaturalSlim® brand. Collectively, these brands have managed to produce $250 million a year in revenue. If you're looking for an ecommerce opportunity with crazy potential, then the rest of this chapter is for you. Before I continue, let me give you an idea of the typical path for this type of business.

First, purchasing inventory itself is a major barrier to entry within the e-commerce world. For example, if you want to sell a beauty line, you cannot simply have one product to compete in this market as you're up against brands that have been around for a long time and have many other complementary products. As a small player with little to no brand awareness, not having a variety of products will limit your ability to sustainably grow without a huge investment.

Now, if you do decide to invest in inventory anyways, let's take a look at what that would take. As an example, a high-quality anti-wrinkle cream can cost $4.75 per unit. However, the minimum order quantity (MOQ) of this product is one thousand units, which comes to a total of $4,750 (not including shipping). So, just like that, one untested and unproven product is going to cost you at least $4,750 to get started. This, of course, doesn't include the cost of marketing, building out websites, storage fees, and so on.

The above example is why many e-commerce brands don't make it, let alone start. It's simply too big of a barrier to entry, and by the time they figure out marketing strategies that work, they've run out of cash.

In 2022, my friend Steven Anderson presented me with an opportunity to join HoneyComm™, a platform which provides a solution to the inventory challenge in e-commerce. It allows access to wholesale prices with a minimum order quantity (MOQ) of one, allowing you to launch your brand without the burden of inventory costs. In other words, instead of having to spend thousands to establish a line of products, HoneyComm™ gives you the freedom to launch your own branded line without paying for inventory until a customer buys your product.

The HoneyComm™ platform offers an ever-growing catalog of supplements and skincare products (consumables) that you can private label. The platform even includes a label-editing tool and an approval process to ensure you're not making any claims that could get you in trouble. You'll even get access to an entire community and a platform that will help you integrate marketing strategies into your newly launched brand.

HoneyComm™ is the entire ecosystem, which includes a private labeling platform, inventory management, fulfillment to customers (they won't ever know there's a company called HoneyComm™ fulfilling their order), inventory storage, multi-channel management, customer service, and more.

This is very similar to drop shipping, but on a different scale with the unique ability to brand these products as your own. Not to mention, all the products (skincare and supplements) are manufactured in the USA and have a 1-3 day delivery window within the USA. International shipping is also an option, opening your sales up to the entire world.

Now, if the idea of creating a new brand seems overwhelming to you, there are ways to make the entire process way easier, especially with the broad availability of AI (Artificial Intelligence). I'll dive more into this subject next, but this technology makes it surprisingly easy to not only build a brand from scratch, but keep it going with endless ideas for marketing, content and more.

Are you ready to take this leap and create your own brand? Scan the QR code below to learn more:

Remember, every journey begins with a single step. Take that step today, and set yourself on the path to becoming an e-commerce entrepreneur. Let's dive into this trillion-dollar market together, and I can't wait to see the success story you'll create.

ARTIFICIAL INTELLIGENCE

Artificial Intelligence (AI) is probably one of the biggest opportunities of this decade. But what is it?

In simple terms, AI is a field of computer science that creates smart machines capable of performing tasks that would normally require human intelligence. These tasks can include things like understanding language, recognizing patterns, solving problems, learning from experience, and making decisions.

Although AI seems new, it isn't. In fact, one of the first AI machines, called the "Logic Theorist," was created in the early 1950's by Allen Newell and Herbert A. Simon. This machine was designed to solve math problems beyond basic calculation. It could think through problems in a way that was similar to how a human would. Really, the only difference between then and now is that AI has become broadly available to the public.

Today, AI can be seen in many aspects of our daily lives, from voice assistants (such as the iPhone's "Siri" or Amazon's "Alexa") to recommendation systems on shopping websites like Amazon. It has also become somewhat of a controversial topic, especially by those who feel threatened by it in some way or by those who simply don't understand it.

And if you happen to be someone who feels a little threatened by it, let me just tell you this: Although AI can do a lot when it comes to repetitive tasks, it cannot replace the full range of human creativity or logic, as it can only do what it is programmed to do.

Regardless, whether we like it or not, AI is here to stay, and those who choose to leverage it will gain an advantage against their competitors. Just like taxis were rendered irrelevant by Uber and Toys "R" Us was decimated by Amazon, AI, along with the ever-growing array of tools released daily, will change the marketplace in a big way.

But let's look at this a little closer. Why are companies like Uber and Amazon so popular? It's because they do an incredible job at two things:

1. Saving time.
2. Making things easier.

AI has done exactly this but on an entirely different level. It can make you significantly faster at what you do if you learn how to use it right. Now, I don't consider myself an AI expert by any means. I'm just an obsessed marketer who gets very excited about opportunities and sharing them with people like you.

So, here's the reality. AI is a tool, and like any other tool, its power lies entirely within the hands of the user. Just like a camera cannot take a beautiful photo without the eye of a skilled photographer, AI cannot do much on its own.

AI also doesn't transform ordinary humans into geniuses. What it can do, however, is make anyone, genius or not, way more efficient at what they do.

First, let's look at a few ways that AI can help you build your dreams faster and more easily than ever before:

TRAINING: AI tools can help you quickly create detailed, step-by-step training manuals to help you do just about anything.

Whether you need guidance on how to create a new website, or you need to give an employee an idea of what they need to do for a particular task, this alone can help tremendously.

RESEARCH: AI tools can speed up the research process by automatically gathering relevant information and even analyzing it for trends and insights. Imagine having a super-smart assistant who can quickly give you all the information you need about your competitors, market or customer preferences.

BRANDING: Creating a brand that stands out is key. AI tools can help you analyze what's trending, suggest logo designs and slogans, and even define who your target audience is.

MARKETING: AI can help you generate customized marketing strategies, as well as give you unlimited ideas for ads based on your specific brand and target audience.

CONTENT CREATION: Creating content, like blog posts or videos, takes time. AI tools can help make this process a lot faster than you ever imagined. Within seconds, you can have a series of emails written, 30 days' worth of social media content ideas (with captions), engaging blogs created, and more. Considering how big of a role content creation plays in the game of business, I'm most excited about this one.

Now let's talk about specific AI tools you can use. As a note, AI is expanding at a very rapid pace, so there's a good chance that some of these tools will be replaced by even better ones within the next year, but this will give you a starting point:

ChatGPT (https://openai.com/blog/chatgpt): An AI tool created by OpenAI (an artificial intelligence research organization) that can generate human-like text. It can be used for gathering information, content creation, proofreading, and more. This tool alone will play a big role in anything you do with AI.

As a note, there is a free (GPT 3.5) and a paid version of ChatGPT (GPT 4). Although the free version is powerful as-is, the paid version will produce better, more accurate results.

Midjourney (www.midjourney.com): One of the more advanced AI tools that can generate images based on what you describe. It can help create a variety of visual content such as logos, images for social media, and more. Note: To access Midjourney, you will need to create a Discord account first (www.discord.com).

Canva (www.canva.com): A graphic design tool that enables users to easily create various types of visual content, such as social media graphics, presentations, posters, and more. More recently, it has incorporated more advanced AI tools that can help you write text (like ChatGPT), generate unique images (like Midjourney), or create entire presentations from an idea.

No matter which AI tool you use, you'll need to become familiar with what's called a "prompt." Simply put, a prompt is what you tell the AI to do or create.

For example, "write a blog about the benefits of AI for a small business owner" would be a prompt used in ChatGPT or within Canva's AI text generation tool. Or, if you were to create an image, "a realistic image of a man walking across the street" would be a prompt you could use in Midjourney or Canva's AI image-generation tool.

Each of these tools will have slight variations in how they are used, but as ChatGPT will likely be at the center of it all, here are a few prompt templates you can try now:

ChatGPT Prompts:

TRAINING:

1. Give me detailed instructions on how to create a [social media platform] account for my business.

   EXAMPLE: Give me detailed instructions on how to create an Instagram account for my business.

2. Write a detailed tutorial on how to [what you're trying to accomplish].

   EXAMPLE: Write a detailed tutorial on how to build my own website economically.

RESEARCH:

1. What would be an ideal audience for [product/service/industry]? Be as detailed as possible.

   EXAMPLE: What would be an ideal audience for gummy vitamins? Be as detailed as possible.

2. Who are the top competitors within the [type of industry] industry? Include their names and websites, and what sets them apart from the rest.

   EXAMPLE: Who are the top competitors within the health supplements industry? Include their names and websites, and what sets them apart from the rest.

Important note: Although ChatGPT can provide information, its knowledge cut-off was in September 2021, so it's always a good idea to verify the information and review more recent sources.

BRANDING:

1. I sell [products/services]. Give me 20 possible brand names that I could use.

   EXAMPLE: I sell a variety of adult gummy vitamins including Vitamin C, Turmeric, Multivitamins, and Vitamin D. Give me 20 possible brand names that I could use.

2. My brand name is [brand name]. Give me 10 detailed logo ideas, including colors I should use.

   EXAMPLE: My brand name is Nature Oasis. Give me 10 detailed logo ideas, including colors I should use.

MARKETING:

1. Write a detailed marketing strategy to rapidly launch a new [industry] business that sells [product/service].

   EXAMPLE: Write a detailed marketing strategy to rapidly launch a new coffee business that sells a variety of premium organic ground coffee and unique coffee mugs.

2. Give me 10 ad ideas including copy and images that I could run to promote [product/service] to [type of audience].

   EXAMPLE: Give me 10 ad ideas including copy and images that I could run to promote vitamin C skin serum to audiences who are somewhat familiar with my brand.

CONTENT CREATION:

1. Give me 30 days' worth of Instagram and Facebook content for my brand, [brand name], which sells [product/services].

   EXAMPLE: Give me 30 days' worth of social media content for my brand, VitaSun which sells a variety of health supplements include collagen, protein powder, multivitamins, etc.

2. Give me 10 ideas for value-based blogs that are somehow related to my brand, [brand name] which sells [products/services].

   EXAMPLE: Give me 10 ideas for value-based blogs that are somehow related to my brand, Art by Tiffany which sells watercolor paintings and art classes.

The above are just a few examples of basic prompts you could try, but learning how to create your own detailed prompts is where the magic happens. Let me demonstrate this.

Let's say you enter this simple prompt into ChatGPT:

PROMPT: Give me an idea for a social media post I could make for my Vitamin C gummy vitamins.

The output would look something like this:

Introducing our latest weapon against pesky colds and flu: Vitamin C gummy vitamins! Say goodbye to sniffles and hello to a stronger immune system with our mouthwatering, orange-flavored gummies packed with the goodness of Vitamin C!

Now, let's provide ChatGPT with more details on what we want:

PROMPT: Give me an idea for a social media post I could make for my Vitamin C gummy vitamins. Include a funny and engaging caption, which social platform(s) it should be posted on and a detailed description of what the image should look like, including dimensions.

The output would look something like this:

Caption: *"When life gives you lemons, grab a handful of these Vitamin C gummies! Say goodbye to sour faces and hello to a daily dose of deliciousness! #CitrusCravings #VitaminCGummyMagic"*

Platform: *Instagram and Facebook*

Image Description:

Dimensions: Square image (1080px by 1080px)

The image should feature a vibrant, colorful background, reminiscent of a sunny citrus orchard. The foreground should showcase a playful arrangement of lemon-shaped Vitamin C gummy candies in various shades of yellow and orange. The gummies should be artfully arranged to form a smiley face, with two larger gummies representing eyes and a curved line of smaller gummies forming a smiling mouth.

The overall composition should be bright, cheerful, and visually appealing, capturing the attention of viewers scrolling through their social media feeds.

Remember to add your brand logo or name discreetly in one corner of the image to reinforce brand recognition.

So, as you can see, the more information you provide the AI, the better the output. In fact, here are a few tips for creating your own prompts:

Be Specific: Say exactly what you want. For example, instead of "write a blog", use "write a blog about the best DIY skincare routines, that includes the use of my Vitamin C serum".

Provide Context: Give some background. For example, instead of "write an email", use "write an email for customers who have visited my website but didn't purchase an item".

Choose the Style: Describe how you want the output to sound/look. For example, if you're using AI to generate text, you can tell it to make it funny, professional, casual, engaging, story-telling, etc.

Control the Length: Ask for a "short answer" or "long answer" to control how much info you get. You can also be specific about the number of words. For example: "make a blog that is at least 1000 words long about the importance of marketing for small businesses."

As a final note, it's important to not only review what these AI tools produce, but to "humanize" them *before* you publish them. As incredible as these tools are, AI is not perfect or error-free. Just like you would check the work of a new employee before you hit "publish," you should review and revise what it produces, as needed.

Hopefully, by this point, you've gotten a few ideas about how you can start incorporating AI into your own business, whether it's for the initial branding process, marketing, training, or anything else.

If you want to learn more about AI, scan the QR code below:

AI, like anything else, requires some practice to learn, but I encourage you to dive in and start learning about it now. Many people haven't yet recognized the huge opportunity that AI presents, so there's still time to leverage this incredible resource and use it to your advantage.

THE NO-COST STARTUP

I wanted to end with an opportunity that is not only timeless but doesn't cost anything to start: becoming a marketer. I might be creating competition for myself by sharing this, but the reality is that learning this skill is essential. It's the one thing that never becomes irrelevant, because whether you are trying to grow your own business or someone else's, you need to become a marketer.

So, how is it that this opportunity can be started with zero money? First, it requires no inventory. Second, all of the information you need is available for free online. Even with a full-time job, you can spend several hours a day consuming content all about this subject. A few content creators that I would personally recommend are Jason Fladlien, Gary Vaynerchuk, Grant Cardone, Rudy Mawer, and Billy Gene. They are all genius marketers who share invaluable insights into how to build agencies and generate revenue through high-quality offers.

You'll also want to spend time learning how social media ad platforms work. If you were to look through YouTube, you'll find endless videos of people walking you through exactly how to navigate these platforms.

After you've spent a good amount of time learning everything you can, you might start to feel confident in your ability to apply some of the things you've learned. When you feel ready, you can start offering your services to businesses for free. Remember, there are plenty of businesses that need and want help with increasing their revenue, some of which are making little to no income. You could start by offering to help them with their social media marketing. Be transparent with them about the fact that you are still learning, but that you want to help them at no cost.

You could say to them, "Hey, I've been studying social media marketing for the last couple of months, and I believe I can help you get more customers and sell more products or services online. I don't want any payment for this. You only have to pay for the advertising directly to the advertising platforms like Google, YouTube, or TikTok, if you're willing to try those out. I would suggest where to advertise, but my work and time will be free. If I'm able to generate incredible results, then we can discuss a potential fee for my time moving forward. Sound good?"

As a note, even with free services, you may still face rejection or skepticism, but don't let that stop you. Keep going until you find that first opportunity. Then, once you find one, work towards producing results. As soon as you've had that first success, you can create a case study that you can use to showcase your work and win over more clients. If you need a few examples of case studies, you'll find a few at www.agmagency.com/case-studies.

To end with a little inspiration, let me share how my journey towards becoming a marketing professional went.

As you know, my journey started with my dad giving me my first opportunity to help him expand his brand, NaturalSlim®. In 2007, when my wife and I presented this idea to him, he accepted it and wrote us a $10,000 check to get started. However, this didn't mean I had full freedom to do whatever I wanted marketing-wise. Considering my history, my dad didn't have a lot of confidence in my marketing abilities at the time. He also wasn't interested in being a "product brand," but rather, an educational brand that helped others take control of their health. So, I was pretty restricted on what I could and couldn't try marketing-wise.

Seven years later, despite making some progress with the brand, we were still struggling financially. While my wife worked on NaturalSlim® full time, I did everything I could to generate the income we needed to keep us afloat. It was around this time that I started learning about how to sell on Amazon. As promising as the information was, I still hadn't earned my dad's trust yet, so I was unable to try any of it with NaturalSlim®.

Not long after was when I decided to jump on the bed sheet opportunity that I mentioned earlier. Before it turned into a multi-million-dollar Amazon brand, Ernesto had been selling these bed sheets on the side of road (literally). Between the information I was learning about selling on Amazon and the fact that the bed sheets required no initial investment, I immediately recognized the huge potential opportunity this presented.

The first thing I did was rebrand these bedsheets as the Cosy House Collection, as they were essentially brandless. Then, we listed them on Amazon. Since this was my own brand, I had full freedom to try any marketing strategy I wanted. Within six months, it was generating $600,000/month in sales.

Now, this business venture was purely intended to help me better support my family. My dad was also completely unaware of what I had been doing with it. One night while he was visiting my home in Texas, I decided to share the sales figures with him. He was very impressed, and it was at that point that I was able to establish the credibility and trust I needed to take NaturalSlim® to the next level.

Like I mentioned earlier, nothing can open the door to new opportunities more than results or success. Want people to start listening to what you have to say? Start working on getting results under your belt, even if it means working for free until you achieve them. In fact, we made little to nothing with NaturalSlim® until 2019 – over a decade after we started.

Why did we persist for so long? Because we saw the potential and it paid off in a big way.

Your journey to success with anything involves two vital elements: the willingness to step outside your comfort zone and a passion for learning.

First, everything you do on a day-to-day basis should contribute in some way to your success. If you're in a challenging situation financially, why spend time on activities that don't improve your circumstances? My advice is to focus obsessively on a single client, brand, job, or opportunity and work on becoming really good at it. This is what will open the door to new and bigger opportunities.

My initial success with one brand established the trust I needed to really take another brand to the next level, which eventually led to even more requests from other brands wanting similar results. Over the years, I've had the honor of helping thousands of clients, content creators, brands, businesses, and organizations with their marketing.

Again, I don't have a college degree or an Ivy League education in marketing, or anything for that matter. It all began with my obsession to capture attention, which is a vital element of success in business.

So, if you are looking for an opportunity to turn your life around, give this one a try. Although it doesn't require any money, it does require your commitment. So, dive into it, understand all these platforms, study as much as you possibly can, and get started. Whether you turn marketing into your life-long passion or not, you'll end up with the tools you need to grow any business.

IF MY GRANDPA WERE ALIVE TODAY

"The opportunity that we have today will not repeat itself."
The Ninja Says

We live in a world full of possibilities, where anyone with access to the Internet can expand their reach and establish an empire at a pace that was once only a dream for our ancestors. I'm sure many of you remember the days before the internet, but now that it has been around for some time, it's very easy to take for granted.

Besides seeing you succeed by applying the information I have shared in this book, my hope is that it will create a sense of urgency in you to act fast. This world is constantly changing, especially technology and the internet. So, the faster you can jump on today's opportunities, the better. Let me tell you a story.

When I was nine years old, my grandfather, a brilliant businessman, came to the house to celebrate. He was extremely proud because, thanks to his marketing efforts, forty-five people entered his toy store that day, twenty-nine of which bought toys from him.

Frank Suarez in front of the Suarez Toy House

This was a huge achievement in his eyes. He spent years of effort, sacrifice, strategizing, analyzing, and investing in marketing to finally generate enough sales to be able to pay his mortgage and support his family.

As young as I was, I celebrated with him that day. Although, I will admit that a happy and content grandfather also meant candy and toys for me. That was three decades ago.

With the effort and sacrifices he made, he was able to celebrate those forty-five prospects in his shop.

The world has changed so much since then. Introducing your brand to the world is easier than ever. In fact, just yesterday I celebrated getting 100,000 prospects who entered just *one* of my online stores. This is only one example of the differences in opportunity today versus only a few decades ago.

Do I consider myself to be smarter than my grandfather? No, but I do consider myself extremely fortunate to have been born in an era where my ability to influence others is not limited to the people in my neighborhood, city, or state. Instead, I can potentially reach the entire world from the comfort of my home. There are no real limitations other than those I place on myself.

I managed to build a company from zero to seven million dollars in just eighteen months. I know a lot of people are going to say, "Ah, of course, but with money, who couldn't? It takes money to make money!"

Would you like to know how much I invested in my business to bring it to those levels? ZERO. Exactly *zero*, not a single penny.

I did this by dramatically increasing my personal value by increasing my knowledge of digital marketing in the modern age, current platforms, and the right strategies that work in today's amazing world of opportunity. I studied for a couple of years incessantly, while at the same time raising three beautiful children with my amazing wife. I studied in the shower, in the car, and in bed, and I took every opportunity to expand my knowledge. Eventually, I made enough money to go to conventions, connect with people of similar thinking, and never rejected an opportunity to expand my knowledge.

With that, I started on my first real journey to apply the knowledge I had acquired and build my bed sheets business, Cosy House Collection, which I later sold for millions. In fact, it's still operating today. But back then, it was my side hustle outside of my nine-to-five that I proudly built from the ground up with my own two hands (often times in my pajamas, I might add).

Ernesto and I building our Cosy House bed sheets brand in my kitchen back in 2014.

I truly believe that anyone can achieve what I have accomplished if they have the *desire* and the *determination to succeed.* Your first step is making the decision that *you* can achieve your dreams while also knowing that you *deserve* to reach your goals.

The entire world is built on decisions. The phone in your hand, the car you drive, the building where you work, the streets you navigate are there and exist because someone along the way, someone like you or me, *decided* to put it there by designing it, creating it, manufacturing it, and finally, making it available to others.

Once you take the first step and make a firm decision to succeed, your next step is to work towards increasing your knowledge of digital media. It is a combination of these two major actions that gave me my success. First, *learn*, and second, *implement*. If we were able to summon my grandfather from beyond the grave and tell him about the possibility of reaching millions of people with little effort, he would probably be skeptical at first. Then, he would immediately demand that we get to work on taking advantage of this opportunity.

If you've gotten this far in the book, it's obvious that you have a dream and the desire to grow. I have many stories to tell about the battles I have won (and lost) over the last four decades of my beautiful life. These successes and failures made me who I am today: someone with a huge desire to see as many people as possible taking advantage of this opportunity that I guarantee *will not repeat itself*.

Our great-grandchildren will be extremely jealous that they could not take advantage of such an incredible and special time where the ability to reach the planet at large and thus, build our dreams was so accessible to everyone.

Someone who has accomplished their dreams for themselves, their group, and the people they care about has obviously made many good decisions along the way, but none of these will ever be bigger and more significant than the decision to *look for* and *walk through* doors of opportunity. With this book, my goal is to guide you towards the creation of a thriving business and, ultimately, a lasting legacy for future generations. The only thing I cannot do is force you to walk through those doors and take the necessary steps to achieve your goals.

So, if you haven't already, get started and start leveraging the opportunities we have now! Your future is waiting.

BONUS CHAPTER: MASTERING CLIENT RELATIONSHIPS

"Communication is the number one art form you must master in marketing and in life."
The Ninja Says

Over the years, I've learned a few vital lessons when it comes to keeping clients satisfied and coming back again and again for our services. It's essential to remember that in the service industry, our primary purpose is to serve our customers.

I often talk to my team about this, especially the artists, who sometimes get upset when a client responds critically to their work. It's important to remember that we are in the service industry and must focus on delivering what the client needs and has paid for, all feelings aside.

It's costly and painful to lose clients or customers, so my hope is to help you save your income and protect the accounts you do have. In fact, it's seven times easier to retain an existing client than to acquire a new one. In the marketing world, I think it's a hundred times easier.

Existing clients provide a steady stream of monthly income. While we may acquire a few new clients every month, it is the regular clients that form the backbone of our revenue. Client retention, therefore, is crucial. Let me tell you a little story about this.

My first client was my father, Frank Suarez. He was a natural communicator and had an amazing ability to attract people. All we had to do was turn on a camera, record what he had to say, and the world loved it. He was the ultimate Content Unicorn.

In 2015, my father suggested that I open a marketing company because a lot of people were asking him what he was doing to accomplish so much success. So, I did! That's when Attention Grabbing Media® (AGM®) was born.

I helped several clients within that first year, but it wasn't until 2016 that I acquired another Content Unicorn, Dr. Eric Berg, who was referred to me by my father. Dr. Berg has been a client ever since. We've helped him conquer the attention game for a long time now. When we first started, he had a few hundred thousand subscribers on YouTube, and now he has over ten million. Across the various social channels, he gets about fifty million video views every month with my distribution strategy.

Something to make note of here is that Dr. Berg consistently creates thirty new pieces of high-quality content every month. We then take that content, turn it into other types of posts (clips, graphics, podcasts, etc.) and create thousands of monthly posts across the various social channels. Like my father, he's an incredible communicator and naturally attracts people, which of course makes our job much easier.

Between my father and Dr. Berg, I was faced with a big problem: I got too lucky. I was spoiled by their ability to attract attention and customers. I was convinced that I could achieve the same levels of success with anyone who wanted to become a "Frank Suarez" or "Dr. Berg", but I was mistaken. People who attract attention at this level are few and far between, hence why I call them "Content Unicorns."

So, this leads me to my first lesson:

Number One: Set the Right Expectations

If someone walks into my office and tells me they want to achieve the same levels of attention as Dr. Berg and I respond with, "Sure! I'll do that in the next three months!" and that doesn't happen, I've set the wrong expectations.

There are some people who will tell you to over-promise and over-deliver. This isn't something I agree with, especially in the marketing world where there are so many factors that can affect the outcome including the brand itself, the audience, the market, the economy, how sales calls are handled, etc.

To set the right expectations, you could tell them something along the lines of, "This is what we've done in the past, and this is what it took to reach the goal. But just so you know, I expect your company to be willing to pay for our services for a year before things start to take off. When you feel like things are getting too complicated or too difficult, remember that the game of building a business and finding a marketing strategy that works is a long-term game. You have to put in the energy, you have to try things out, and you have to work with us until something clicks."

Setting the correct expectations from the beginning will open the door to referrals, longer-term clients, and a reduced churn rate.

So, let's say that you now have a client. How do you keep them? Let's look at the second lesson.

Number Two: Maintain Consistent Communication

Communication alone can solve so many things, especially in the world of business. If you stop communicating with your clients, they start to wonder what's happening with the service they paid for. And even if you are falling behind on the expectations you set in the past, you can buy yourself some time.

This has to be something that is done consistently with your clients, whether it's via phone calls, emails, texts, chat or any other communication tool you use. When you do this, a client will feel like you've assumed ownership over their brand, their products, and ultimately, their success. Now, let's go over the third and final lesson in keeping clients on board.

Number Three: Get Results

I know this might sound obvious, but getting results is extremely important. Not only will results buy you time across the board, but they can even forgive insufficient communication or that you set the wrong expectations at some point.

At the end of the day, what your clients want are results. Any sane client will value effective performance and is not likely to cut ties with someone who consistently meets or exceeds what they promise to do. So, focus on doing everything you can to get results.

These three lessons, especially in this sequence, are the most important aspects to focus on when it comes to servicing clients. Here they are again:

1. **Set the Right Expectations**
2. **Maintain Consistent Communication**
3. **Get Results**

It doesn't matter what industry you are in. Start by letting them know what the process looks like (this is part of setting the right expectations). Communicate with them consistently to let them know what's happening. And finally, make sure you're doing everything you can to get the results you promised.

Over the years, I've made it an obsession to not only deliver expectations, but to go above and beyond. This has always led to a constant flow of referrals and new clients. In fact, even Dr. Berg, one of today's biggest influencers, recently got on the phone with me to help convince a client that hiring my agency was the correct thing to do for their brand. The next day, they signed the contract and became a client of AGM®. Did Dr. Berg expect a commission? Not at all. He simply wanted to help us grow because we've taken thorough responsibility for his brand and his growth. This is something he has helped us with many times and is purely driven by the results we've produced for him over the years.

Results are what will create your top advocates who will bring in more business than any advertising could ever produce. By following these steps in this sequence, I've seen repeated success. With it, I've been able to grow my organization to the levels I'm at today. My hope is that it can do the same for you.

BONUS CHAPTER: BUILDING YOUR TEAM

"Your ability to grow is going to be directly proportionate to your ability to delegate. It is your responsibility as a leader to show your people what is possible."
The Ninja Says

As I've mentioned before, I don't consider myself a "self-made" success, but a "team-made" success. I truly wouldn't be where I am today without my team. The reality is, there is only so much you can do on your own. There will be a point where you realize you need an extra hand or two, which is what I'll be sharing in this chapter.

Today, we have hundreds of employees across multiple organizations, but it all started with one. The first employee I hired was for my bed sheet brand, Cosy House Collection. At the time, we were selling about $600,000 a month and growing rapidly. Between this business and what I was doing with NaturalSlim®, I was becoming very overwhelmed with the workload I had.

Before you start hiring anyone, there are two things you will need to come to terms with. First, you need to accept that you do need help, which I know can be easier said than done. Second, you need to accept that no one will be as passionate as you are about your business. In other words, you won't likely find someone who can do what you do as well as you do. Once you get over that fact, it becomes easier to bring in staff and go through the process of making them valuable to your organization.

It can be frustrating working with others, especially if there are areas that you feel very skilled in. In my experience, marketing is one of my strongest skills and it's hard to pass the torch to someone else who might not think the same way I do. Regardless, I know that if I don't get help, I won't be able to keep expanding.

So, once you're ready, what now? What type of employee should you hire? Where do you find them? One of the greatest things about this era we live in is that it's easier than ever to find employees, locally and around the world.

Over the last couple of decades, it has become increasingly popular to hire what's called a virtual assistant (VA). A VA is someone who can work for you from anywhere in the world and is often skilled in a variety of responsibilities from customer service and marketing to administrative tasks and accounting.

This will likely be one of the first employees you will want to hire. You can delegate anything to them that you think they can handle so that you can focus on the bigger picture for your brand.

As far as *where* to look for your own VA, there are a few I can suggest:

20Four7VA.com
Upwork.com
OnlineJobs.ph
Freeup.net

These are just a few, but there are several others like them. Many of the VAs you'll find are based in the Philippines. In fact, a good portion of my current team is from the Philippines. Not only are they willing to match our schedule, but they are some of my best employees that help me with marketing, design, video editing, and more. They're also all hard workers, loyal and speak fluent English.

Many of them have also been trained specifically to work with American companies, so when you bring them on board, they'll already know how to communicate and work professionally. Whether you need help with editing content, copywriting, managing emails, creating lead generation funnels, building websites, or scheduling content, they can do it.

Finding employees overseas is also an economical way to get the help you need, as the economy and cost of living in some of these countries is very different from what we're used to. For example, the average household income in America (as of 2022) is somewhere around $78,000 per year. In the Philippines, it's closer to $20,000 per year.

To speed up the selection process, you can create a quiz to filter those who are interested in the positions you need to fill. This can help you spot those who are already skilled versus those who are new. ChatGPT can be helpful in generating the questions and answers for this. For example, you could type in the following as a ChatGPT prompt:

PROMPT: Create a twenty-question quiz with multiple choice answers to find out the current skill level of a social media marketer. Indicate which one is the correct answer.

Hiring from outside of the US can be a controversial topic for some but here's how I see it. First, every one of my remote employees makes more money working with my company than they would working within their own country. They're able to buy things that their country's average wage wouldn't allow them to, such as cars, homes, etc.

So, if you're feeling a little overloaded or limiting yourself because you don't have time, just know this: Your ability to grow is directly proportional to your ability to delegate. The moment you start delegating, you'll be able to start expanding.

My first hire was in 2014 and has been with me ever since. He's an incredible member of our team and provides an enormous amount of value to the organization. He has also been growing personally within the company.

You can find incredible people from all over the world and bring them into your team. They're everywhere: Philippines, Mexico, Venezuela, Costa Rica, Colombia, and other countries, all looking for opportunities. Many of these people will be dedicated and loyal to you and your mission and may even become an extension of your family.

This is how I've grown my team and they are a big reason behind my success.

FINAL THOUGHTS FROM THE NINJA

"Failure is an integral part of the path to success. Embrace every failure as the lesson that will make you wiser and get you closer to your goals."
The Ninja Says

I sincerely want to thank you for the time you've taken to explore this book. I truly hope that this book has helped and inspired you in some way, and that you are not only now ready to take action but have been doing so throughout this book. I've been a passionate educator for many years, and it has been a major goal of mine to take the enormous amount of practical knowledge of life, personal development, and marketing magic and turn it into a book with the potential to help others and get them started on their own journey where they can truly discover their full potential. Most people have a very limited view of marketing as a subject and just as a word. They usually just equate it to strategies that help you generate sales and revenue, but marketing is so much more than that.

Marketing includes *you* as a person. Before the doors of opportunity open, you must market yourself, you must sell yourself and your own ability to impact others. Marketing presents a path for personal development that will help any individual get attention that will inevitably lead to more opportunities.

In the business world, marketing is what allows a brand to immortalize itself. It is the one thing that will provide the oxygen necessary for a brand to not only sustain itself but to expand.

Marketing is not only magic, but it is applicable to every aspect of life. Even when it comes to finding your ideal match, you need to market yourself, or they won't ever get to know you. It is also a big responsibility. If you truly believe your products and services can improve a person's life in some way, you have a responsibility. That aspect of their lives is in your hands. The longer you take to reach people, the longer they will continue having problems you could have resolved for them with your valuable products and services. This is quite a responsibility, especially if you're like me and you truly care about helping people and making a difference in their lives through your amazing Superpower.

Take *you* for example. I'm confident that just because you got this far in the book, your life will dramatically improve even if you only apply some of what I've shared. I know this for a fact because this book is filled not with opinions, but with universal facts that anyone can prove to themselves such as acquiring knowledge, leading with value, leveraging today's modern platforms to get attention, understanding that capturing attention leads to revenue, etc.

How many more people out there could use the knowledge in this book to improve their current scene? How many people have I failed to reach? How many people could have a dramatically higher quality of life for themselves, their families, and their employees, but I simply have not reached them? Do you see? This keeps me awake at night, and it's called *responsibility*.

Marketing, getting the attention of people, and creating opportunities to sell your products and services is a major responsibility and should be a priority for any business or mission who wishes to impact the world in a big way.

My vision for "Marketing Magic" is that it will tangibly help anybody who has the desire to impact the world and leave a legacy.

Are you a person who wants to be proud of what you accomplished? Do you want to have something for future generations to benefit from? I wrote this book for you. I believe I'm giving you strategies that will enable you to succeed massively. I want to know your stories and hear about your successes *and* your challenges.

The social media world is going to be very different in the future. New platforms are going to emerge, and we'll have an even more established internet world. There won't be a big separation between e-commerce and commerce, especially with people consuming content on a very large scale.

Just during the COVID pandemic, we saw a major transition into a very digital era. Just during that time, there was a massive acceleration of doctor visits over video calls, while many others gathered to learn, sing, and socialize without ever leaving their home. There's going to be a lot more changes, and technology will keep on evolving even faster and faster.

People will be more efficient across the board, as we're witnessing right now with the evolution and broad availability of artificial intelligence for the general public. I can't wait to see what the world presents to us. And if you understand the value of *opportunities*, which I'm sure you do by now, you're bound to find an ever-growing number of them as time progresses.

I'm so grateful for life in general. I'm grateful to have a body that works. I'm very grateful to work with friends surrounding me. I'm grateful that I have a darn good mind when it comes to business and marketing.

Of course, you know I'm grateful for my family, who has been my primary source of inspiration every step of the way.

I'm also grateful that I know how to create my own economy, despite what's happening in the world. Instead, I'm able to create an environment where I can succeed no matter what. With this book, I'm arming you with the same tools I've used all along. I created my own success along the way. You will too.

Every single difficulty I faced in my life has made me who I am today. Understanding what it's like to have nothing is a very, very powerful force. Understanding what it's like to be broke is something that really motivates me and inspires me every day. One of the biggest challenges I've faced as a father of four kids is making sure that they understand what it's like to win. If you're born into privilege, it's a different path than learning how to build success from the bottom. My failures and disappointments made me stronger each time. I use those experiences every single day to keep on succeeding at a whole new level.

My biggest wish for myself and for you is that you accomplish freedom and achieve happiness. And for me, freedom and happiness can be expressed this way: freedom to do what I want to do, and freedom to *not* do what I *don't* want to do. That for me is the end goal of all of this, and that's true happiness. When you're able to go to work and life doing those things that you *want* to do, you're happy and you've won. It doesn't matter what that is… when you have to force yourself to be somewhere that you don't want to be, that results in unhappiness.

Life should never be solely about working for retirement or working to achieve financial freedom. Life is too precious and too beautiful for that. When I wake up every morning, I ask myself, "Am I doing something today I'd rather not do?" And if the answer is "yes", I know one thing for a fact: I have to keep working harder until I can one day respond to that question with a resounding "no."

I'll let you in on a little secret. I've been answering no to that question for quite a few years now. I get to work excited every day. I love raising my family. I enjoy every business I'm a part of and every group I'm involved in. Just like kids love playing video games, I love playing the game of life every day, and I don't ever take for granted how blessed I've been over the years. If I ever wake up feeling unmotivated about my day, I sure as heck know I better learn something new that day, because it's time to expand into a new area, and it's time to produce at a higher level.

My daily motivation is the journey. I love every step of it. I thrive when I'm playing the game, and no matter how great the accomplishments are, I always look for more. Why isn't it ever enough?

Simple. Because I love what I do, and why would you ever stop doing something you love so passionately? I can assure you of one thing: I will be doing this marketing and business game until the day this body fails me. This switch that turned on years ago does not have an off position, and that's my wish for you.

Do something that motivates and inspires you every single day. Do something that makes you feel proud. Do something that you don't feel you will burn out from or makes you yearn for the day you're able to finally retire from. Do something you passionately love so much that you know, deep down, you will happily keep doing it until the very end. This is an absolute recipe for massive success and an inevitable legacy.

If you have a great business, and you're passionate about spreading your message and applying the principles detailed in this book, feel free to reach out. Let's find out if we're a good fit for each other. Before we connect, let me tell you about my perfect client.

The perfect client for me is a person who really understands the game of business and the game of marketing, but who is not desperate for immediate results. They understand what the journey looks like. They're willing to play the game and be a partner in the process with me and my team as we create strategies that help them get massive attention.

They're dedicated to putting their own resources, human and otherwise, into their own business so they can build a legacy. The perfect client for me is really interested in creating an impact, someone who wants to change people's lives with their products and services. They feel a responsibility to humanity, and they want to create a better world. I want to work with someone like that every day. Like me, they are *dreamers*, but even more than that, they are *doers*.

If you decide to reach out to me, be sure to tell me that you want to know what special opportunities I can offer to people who are not only able to DREAM, but who are able to DO.

Only someone who has made it to this last paragraph will know to ask. And only someone who asks will know what it is that awaits.

I invite you to meet not only me but my whole team at Attention Grabbing Media®. I'm opening a door here, and I'm *so* curious to see who comes through. I hope it's YOU. Send a text message to 813-212-2196 (if you are in the US) or send me a DM on Instagram (@mrmanuelsuarez). You can also email me at manuel@manuelsuarez.com. See you on the other side.

HOW I BECAME "THE MARKETING NINJA"

Over the years, I've become known as the "Marketing Ninja." As a born and raised Puerto Rican, I'm definitely not a fourteenth-century Japanese mercenary trained in martial arts. But let me tell you a little about why this became part of who I am.

If you Google the word "ninja," you'll find this definition: "a person who excels in a particular skill or activity." For my entire life, I have strived to be a winner. Despite some of the pitfalls I've had along the way, I truly wanted to excel and be the *best* at anything I did. Being second place was my greatest nightmare.

As you know by now, my father was my hero. Always was and always will be. When I was younger, my father would come back from his business trips to Japan or Taiwan, and he would share his collection of Japanese Ninja or Samurai swords with me. These were some of my favorite core memories growing up, and sparked an overall admiration for Eastern culture.

Fast forward about fifteen years, a movie called *The Last Samurai* became an all-time favorite of mine. Another decade later, I met one of my first mentors, Ben Cummings, who would often introduce powerful marketing strategies with, "This is ninja!" As Ben was a big part of the beginning of my career in marketing, this one really stuck with me.

Based on these experiences, I decided to make "ninja" part of my personal branding. It started as "The Facebook Ninja", since that was the first platform I really excelled at. Over time, as my knowledge and experience in marketing grew, it morphed into "The Marketing Ninja."

Today, you'll find ninjas incorporated into the overall branding of my marketing company, from the walls and artwork in our office to the emails and content we create.

So, as you work towards your own goals, feel free to assume the mentality of a ninja to help you strive for excellence and perseverance in everything you do.

MEET MANUEL

Usually there is a section in a book called "About the Author." But, since I'm a marketer, not an author per se, and since you've already read all about me, the editors of this book decided to conduct interviews with a few of my longest-running team members and their perspective of who I am.

THE INTERVIEWS

You've already read the chapter from Manuel that covers the importance of building your team. Now you get to hear from Manuel's team themselves. What struck us the most when we interviewed each of the eight team members, as well as Manuel's wife, was the sincerity of the responses. No one was putting on a performance to enhance their leader's reputation.

Now you have the chance to meet the actual team that Manuel speaks so passionately about. Maybe this will inspire you to continue building or expanding your own team too.

Here is who we interviewed:

Chief Marketing Officer, **Jorge** Rodriguez
Chief Operations Officer, **Ollie** Rodriguez
Chief Administrative Officer, **Ernesto** Barrientos
Special Projects Officer, **Jules** De Armon
Creative Director, **Jimmy** Stearns
Senior Graphic Designer, **Dolf** Ponsaran

Customer Service Supervisor, **Rain** Ponsaran
Senior Video Editor, Joel Ceneciro (**JC**) Jr.
Wife, Gabriela (**Gaby**) Suarez

The first set of questions was just for getting acquainted:

Q: What's your name, your position, and what do you actually do?

Jorge: CMO. I oversee all the marketing for different accounts, including hands-on activities. The ones I'm closest to are non-Amazon lead generation and eCommerce. I also market for the AGM® Agency as well as Manuel's personal brand.

Ollie: COO. I handle all operations on a daily basis.

Ernesto: CAO. I'm in charge of finances, and legal matters, plus sales, accounting, and QuickBooks. I also occasionally work on special projects to increase production.

Jules: Special Ops Ninja. I do a variety of things, but I often work directly with VIPs, as well as some of the top-priority, "figure-it-out" types of projects for AGM®.

Jimmy: Creative Director. I help coordinate audio and video for AGM® and Manuel Suarez along with recording, distributing, and directing the content for both brands. What I strive to do is capture Manuel in the best possible way to ensure he is able to accomplish building his legacy and spreading his knowledge to help the masses.

Dolf: Senior Graphic Designer. I design graphics, logos, and branding guidelines for various AGM® clients and for Manuel Suarez.

Rain: Customer Service Supervisor. I oversee and manage the customer service department for both Manuel's personal brand and Amazon clients. My role involves providing training and support to the customer service team, monitoring and evaluating customer interactions to maintain high standards, and handling escalated inquiries or complaints that frontline representatives cannot resolve.

JC: Senior Video Editor. I edit videos mostly for the AGM® brand.

Q: How did you meet Manuel? How long have you known him? How long have you worked for him?

Jorge: He's my brother-in-law, so maybe seventeen years. Ollie is my younger brother and I've known Ernesto since I was fourteen. I've been here since the beginning since we started AGM® together. We have very similar personalities and the same inclination to just "figure it out," no matter what kind of adventure we've gotten ourselves into.

Ollie: We're family. He's married to my sister, Gabriela. I've known him over seventeen years and worked with him for more than ten years in one way or another.

Ernesto: Jorge and Ollie and I had been friends and business partners for twenty-five years. Jorge and Ollie are brothers, so when Manuel married their sister Gabriela, he became part of the group. I met him fifteen years ago when he was working with his dad selling cell phones. I started working with him in 2011, so eleven years now.

Jules: He's my cousin, so I've known him for most of my entire life. I've been working with him for over four years but worked with him and Gaby for a while in 2012 when NaturalSlim® was just starting to take off in the USA.

Jimmy: I originally found out about Manuel through one of his employees in 2019. She introduced me to his content and his company, AGM® Marketing. Then, in 2020 I became a remote employee of his shortly before the pandemic hit. It wasn't until 2021, that I officially met Manuel in person when I visited Florida for AGM®'s grand opening for their state-of-the-art building. It was like meeting a celebrity, because I was used to seeing him through the computer screen or on my phone in so many videos. He had such a great influence on me that I was honestly a bit star struck when I met him finally.

Dolf: I've known and worked for Manuel since 2017.

Rain: I had the opportunity to meet Manuel through a friend who recommended me to work as an Amazon customer service representative at AGM®. It has been over five years since I first got to know Manuel

JC: Manuel was my first employer, so I met him when I was chosen for the job around 2017.

Now that the getting acquainted questions were out of the way, we dove into the "meat" of "Meet Manuel." You'll find it interesting how often each team member came up with almost the same answer as the others.

Q: What makes Manuel different from other leaders you've known, worked for, or observed?

Jorge: He's very intense in the sense of being willing to push to meet a target. When he gets an idea in his head, you either get on the train or get out of the way. Tenacity all the way.

Ollie: He really cares about making others succeed in life. He really wants to help his staff, help them grow, and assist them in resolving their problems. Has an inherent desire to help the people around him. Unselfish. Somebody you can rely on at a personal level.

Ernesto: Three main things: 1. He really cares about his staff. 2. He sets BIG goals. 3. He will never stop or give up until he achieves the target.

Jules: Probably the biggest thing is his trust in me, which took some getting used to. Not that previous employers didn't trust me, but I wasn't really pushed to grow with other employers. Naturally I'm a go-getter, but I don't think I've grown as fast anywhere else as I have working with Manuel. I remember early on, he'd give me some task that I had very little to no experience with. When I'd doubt my ability to do something, he would just say "I trust you." And I'd do it. Sometimes I'd even surprise myself. Over time, my confidence really grew.

Jimmy: I've worked many jobs and never once encountered someone as passionate as Manuel when it comes to ensuring his team's success. He is devoted to maintaining his staff's satisfaction with their work and providing them with the opportunity to learn and expand. He emphasizes the development of skills and knowledge, enabling them to continue doing what they love with the opportunity to increase their pay at a much faster rate than I have ever witnessed before. He's the ideal leader you'd want to run your company and I am extremely lucky to have him as mine.

Dolf: He never sleeps. Haha.

Rain: Manuel has a great ability to motivate and inspire all of us. He's also very passionate about what he does.

JC: He's very obsessed when it comes to getting something done.

Q: What is the working environment like on a day-to-day basis?

Jorge: Manuel is very intense in that he's willing to push to meet a target. When he sets a goal, you need to keep up. Keep up your own tenacity.

Ollie: Marketing is a fast-paced sometimes hectic industry. Things change so rapidly, and you're dealing with people's money, and you want to do the best you can. You could compare it to the floor of the stock market. Except you have a little more control than in the stock market.

Ernesto: Busy! There are always new projects. A lot of creativity and overall, a *fun* environment.

Jules: It's always intense. Never boring. I've been here for over four years, and it feels like at least ten. Having worked at slow, boring jobs in the past, I definitely prefer this pace. Considering the nature of the marketing industry, it can be challenging some days. But in the end, you just get stronger because of it.

Jimmy: It›s fast-paced. I mean, literally every day is full throttle. Marketing changes so fast with the trends and technology that you really have to go at a thousand miles per hour to stay ahead. It's also equally challenging and rewarding. Every single day is so different compared to the last; it's very hard to get bored. I also find that I learn something new every day at AGM® just because of the fast paced environment, but I also get a lot of pressure to produce results, and I absolutely love that aspect about working here.

JC: Lots of pressure when there's a new launch, but otherwise smooth sailing!

Q: What aspect of Manuel's character do you believe makes him so successful?

Jorge: Probably his competitive nature. He just wants to reach the target and win, no matter what it is. As far as he's concerned, there's nothing that isn't a game.

Ollie: His tenacity. Persistence on a given course. I've seen him work on a goal for years before it finally comes to fruition. His tenacity can pay off in a very big way. I would also say his willingness to put himself in uncomfortable positions makes him successful.

Ernesto: Two things: intelligence and building relationships. He's very intelligent. When he starts a new campaign for a client or potential client, it's pure GENIUS.

Jules: Probably his creativity and persistence. No matter what, he might get shot down, but he gets right back up and continues. He can always come up with something to get past any barrier.

Jimmy: It's his genuine desire to help everyone succeed that sets him apart. Manuel wants everyone around him to improve their lives and to evolve into the best version of themselves. Coupled with his competitive nature and unyielding drive to win, these traits make him exceptionally successful and impactful. It doesn't hurt that he's a super nice guy too.

Dolf: He never stops learning.

Rain: His commitment to helping others make their businesses successful and his will to push forward.

JC: Obsessed with getting things done, always learning, always making new friends, very direct, sincere, and he's a big dreamer.

Q: What separates Manuel from other marketing gurus or trainers?

Jorge: He's a contrarian, in the sense that he doesn't just do what everyone else does. He does something different and that's why people are attracted. We're a marketing agency (used to be a Facebook marketing agency). Everybody sells courses on things like paid ads. Manuel talks about how to do things for free, providing value. And he actually did do whatever he was talking about, instead of just promoting it.

Ollie: Depends on which gurus. Some will only give advice but never built anything themselves. Manuel built multiple million-dollar businesses. Amazon, supplements, agency, and still manages over two hundred and fifty employees. He has a track record of always giving advice. There was a lot of implementation as he grew those businesses. He *had* to be a practitioner. That's a lot of hours of work at a craft. And don't forget his IQ. Lastly, his IQ sets him apart from any other pretenders.

Ernesto: He learns more than anyone I know, and he tests aggressively. He tests what he learns.

Jimmy: Probably his ability to just figure things out. Manuel delved into everything on his own, studying like crazy, and gaining hands-on experience to determine the best methods. He had failed many times until he succeeded, and continually adapted and learned along the way. He can speak from experience, you know? Kinda like an army general who has served on the frontlines in their youth, ran through the trenches, and came back with the battle experience to lead the troops to victory. Except we're talking about marketing, not war. Haha.

Dolf: His extensive industry experience, knowledge of the latest marketing trends and strategies, and a genuine passion for helping individuals and businesses succeed is what sets him apart.

Rain: Just that he never sleeps and is always learning more.

JC: I find his results more impressive than others in the industry.

Q: What story would you like to share that demonstrates Manuel's qualities?

Jorge: When we were starting out around 2017, the first few months going, we're still trying to figure each other out, personalities, and that kind of stuff. He says, "I need you to help me figure out something," and I say, "Oh no, it can't be done." I was very confident it couldn't be done. He basically figured it out with just Google and YouTube and came back and said, "It CAN BE DONE. You can't close the door. Everything is figure-out-able." It changed the way I work in general. There's always a solution.

Jules: A few years ago, we were about to launch a brand-new service called "The Catapult System", which is an Amazon product ranking service. The Catapult System itself was mostly built using ManyChat, which is a platform that allows businesses to create chatbots for messaging apps like Facebook Messenger, so they can automate conversations with their customers or followers. Not only was this a complicated and extensive service, ManyChat was still fairly new to me. By the time I joined in to help launch this, we had maybe two weeks to figure out the intricacies of the system itself, how we were going efficiently deliver it to potentially hundreds of people, how we were going to promote it, etc. It was intense!

Between myself and another employee, we had many 10-12 hour days figuring it out. And believe me when I say… I was uncertain about so many things (considering it was my first launch AND I was no expert in the main platform we were using, ManyChat). Time and time again Manuel would just tell me, "I trust you." Just that was enough to feel confident in the decisions I was making to make that launch a success. And it was exactly that! I don't know for sure, but I'm fairly certain it was one of the top-producing launches we ever did!

While working with Manuel over the last few years, I've continued to have similar experiences, all of which just boosted my confidence in myself every time. This has even positively affected other areas of my personal life where my own uncertainty would normally get in the way. Instead, I just push those uncertainties aside and do whatever it is that I set out to do.

Jimmy: I think one of the best ones is when Manuel decided to give out the Facebook Master's Course for free during the pandemic to help people learn and understand how to use social media marketing to improve their lives. There were hundreds of video testimonials that came in from that. I think that it's really cool how he just gave away all his hard work to the world for free just so that it could help others improve their lives.

Q: What's the most important thing you've learned working with Manuel? And how have you changed in working with him? How are you different now? What is your biggest accomplishment or contribution to the team?

Jorge: I learned "Don't give up on a target. Don't be closed to solutions." I'm always looking for the answers now… 10x more than I used to. I'm always thinking about keeping the customer happy… doing more than is expected… working with the attitude of wowing them, even if it goes outside the scope of work. Recently, Manuel assigned me an account. I'm not an account manager, but he said we need to personally do this and blow them out of the water. I said OK, and the first month I doubled the result they were expecting. Now, we double it every month, so we scaled them beyond what they thought was possible. They were very happy about this!

Ollie: I've learned to be willing to risk what you have for what you don't have. I'm willing to risk more. I have an improved work ethic. I would say overall that I now have the desire for growth and expansion constantly there. It's contagious. Ambition is contagious.

I've been able to build systems that contribute and allow us to grow and hire more people, get more clients, and increase our revenue. Building systems that allow for expansion is what I do all day. And I love it.

Ernesto: I've learned to walk the line. When I have to get some production done, or do something to kind of check it out, test it out, put myself in the customer's viewpoint and figure out if they will receive something done professionally, I'm flat on it. My eyes are now open to the fact that you can figure things out. A lot of people tell you it's impossible, but that's a lie. And I love getting other staff members to realize their potential. That's one of Manuel's Superpowers and main virtues.

Jules: Working with Manuel has really taught me about the importance of *speed*. He puts a lot of emphasis on speed of the flow of all the particles in the organization, which I think is one of the main things that sets this agency apart from others. Manuel will see an opportunity and have us jump on it ASAP.

Also, in the past, I've been a bit of a pushover. I'd often be afraid to voice my opinions about something, even if I did have the experience to back it up. That has reversed… I have the confidence in myself to tell a client I don't recommend something. My confidence has gone up *a lot*.

Jimmy: To be results driven, to take action, and shoot for the stars. Basically, if I want it, all I have to do is go for it and it will become a reality. It's powerful man. I went from being self-doubting, unsure of what to do with my life, and pretty much losing at the game of life to being very confident in my abilities, having direction in my life, and progressing towards a better future for myself and my family. It's been quite a transformation. If you met me in 2019 versus who I am today, you would not believe that we are the same person. I do owe that to Manuel for pushing me to be a better version of myself.

My biggest accomplishment has been the ability to continually evolve AGM®'s creative assets to become better and unique compared to the competition. I think this is how an agency can stand out in the sea of competition, you know?

I have also helped build studios for Manuel's friends and clients, which have been really cool to see come to life. Even helping with the setup and livestreaming of all events and workshops at the AGM® headquarters has been an honor to be a part of.

Dolf: He has always said that the moment you stop learning is the moment you stop earning. Over these last several years, I've been continually pushed to grow and learn something new. I think my biggest accomplishment is creating the AGM® ninja lab logo and a flyer I created for NaturalSlim®, which I think they are still using today.

Rain: That you have to figure things out and work with speed. The biggest change I've seen in myself is that my social anxiety has improved a lot. I think what I'm most proud of is the fact that he trusts me to assist him during important webinars or meetings.

JC: You have to be dedicated to your goals and work toward them every day. Generally, I'm a pretty relaxed type of person, but since working with Manuel, I've developed a new mindset that I like to call "beast mode." My biggest accomplishment was leading a team of editors to finish Manuel's first course, The Facebook Master's Course which consisted of 48 hours of content.

Q: What do you think is Manuel's biggest accomplishment?

Jorge: His family business, being able to scale that from nothing to nine figures. Nobody had that dream when they first started. Nonexistent when they started.

Ollie: What he's the proudest of would be how his dad admired his skills. He had to earn that. Frank was his biggest mentor. Also building an agency with over one hundred employees. He did that on his own with nobody's help, no funding, and without a mentor. He said, "I'm going to build an agency. I don't know what I'm doing." He just went for it. Five years later, with three, back to back "Inc 5000" awards, industry awards and recognitions, and connections with top marketers all over the world, he more than hit that goal.

Ernesto: Building a marketing team of over one hundred and twenty people.

Jules: Growing AGM® to the size it is. Getting the actual incredible building itself to be a reality. We didn't have much of an office when I started. What we have now looks so polished and professional. The fact that he grew AGM® to this point is very impressive.

Jimmy: How he helped to build up his dad's company and how he has continued his dad's legacy in such a unique and impactful way that helps people all over the world. It's been over 2 years since his father passed away and they are still spreading his knowledge everywhere and growing his company. That's just incredible, man. And what it really is all about is helping people do better, feel better, and be the best version of themselves... that's what his dad did and is still doing because of Manuel. It's incredible.

Dolf: How he has helped inspire his employees, including myself, to reach their true potential.

Rain: His commitment to constant growth and expansion, for himself and his team.

JC: Successfully figuring out the most effective marketing strategies today.

Q: What phrase or mantra that Manuel repeats often sticks with you the most?

Jorge: There's no such thing as failure. That's the way he acts.

Ollie: You don't know what you don't know.

Ernesto: A lot of phrases put pressure on me to get production done, and I go ehhh… don't stop until you get it done. Don't go to sleep until you get it completed.

Jules: Omnipresence. As a brand, you must be everywhere the eyeballs of the world are. It's directly connected to the amount of income you can potentially generate.

Jimmy: I think one that he has said many times over that sticks out in my mind is the Seneca quote, "Luck Is What Happens When Preparation Meets Opportunity."

Dolf: Figure it out!

Rain: Figure it out.

JC: Always be learning and doing things with speed.

Q: What one word (or words) do you feel best describes Manuel?

Jorge: COMPETITIVE. Altitude. Networker. Power. Chess. (Always thinking 3 moves ahead.)

Ollie: PERSISTENT. Marketer. Salesman. Unselfish. Loving. Friend.

Ernesto: CARE. Production. Productivity. Push-through.

Jules: PERSISTENT. Creative. Courageous. Strong-willed. Games. Intense.

Jimmy: Ninja. THE Marketing Ninja.

Dolf: Curious.

Rain: Forward-thinker.

JC: Family man.

Q: What else would you like to share about Manuel that we didn't cover already?

Jorge: One of his best qualities outside of work is that he loves his kids and his family… he'd do anything for them… for all of us.

Ernesto: Just a quick story. When we were first getting started with the Amazon bedding brand, we were in Manuel's kitchen in our pajamas, and Manuel told me that we were going to make this brand look like it was a worldwide brand with thousands of employees, even if that wasn't the reality yet. One year later, we were selling $600K a month. Crazy to think about how far we've come!

***

When interviewing Manuel's wife Gaby, what was clearer than ever was her determination to give thoughtful, insightful, candid answers. She would often take several moments to consider her answer as if she hadn't thought of some of the questions before. Here's what Gabriela (Gaby) Suarez had to say:

My formal title is Executive Director at NaturalSlim®, and I'm in charge of the whole organization. I met Manuel in 2003 during a period when I was in a time of "self-improvement," and when I met Manuel, I could immediately notice that he was a very sincere person when it comes to showing his feelings. You could see in his eyes and smile exactly how he feels. He's very communicative and doesn't hold back. He's very direct. We married in 2006. I think we've been together almost twenty years now.

What makes Manuel different from other leaders I've known is that he's extremely transparent.

He's extremely sincere in his intentions with people as a leader or businessperson. When he says, "Dr. Berg is a powerhouse, and I'm going to spread him all over the world," he doesn't say it to pump up the client, he says it because he really means it and will stay up until midnight to make it happen. Business is not what drives him. Connection with people is what drives him. I get to see what he's willing to put on the table to connect. That's so different from others. He understands business and money of course, but what drives him is to connect to people and support them to have success. He really enjoys the success of his clients, it's the fuel that drives him.

The aspect of Manuel's character that makes him so successful is obsession. No, I take that back. The right word is "relentless". Relentless in the face of opposition. Even if he has to quiet himself down and go in some other direction first, through the side or back doors if he wants something, he's relentless, *even* when it's for someone else.

What separates Manuel from other marketing gurus, is that yes, he's a marketer, but above that, he's a teacher. He will hold *nothing* back when it comes to teaching. We're in the service industry, the intellectual property industry, but he has no desire to hold back what he knows. He's not protective of his knowledge. "How can I possibly teach more people more of what I know?" That's his philosophy. He believes you become an opinion leader on a subject and give it away for free.

Before we started the agency, he was doing very well with some clients who paid him extremely well. He had recently sold his original Amazon brand, and he said, "I'm going to start an agency." I asked him what for. I told him we were making more money than we need. We work from home and we were golden. Why on earth would he want to build an agency?

"I want to work with *people*."

"We're going to have to invest all the money you just made selling our business, and now our monthly income will be reduced. Why on earth? We're finally the most secure we've ever been."

"But that doesn't make me happy. I need to have a group. Don't worry, we'll make it back and then some. I need to work with people."

That story shows me the kind of man I'm married to.

What's the most important thing I've learned working with Manuel? I've learned how to have integrity. I've learned that money is trash in business and that relationships are everything. Getting to pick and choose who you work with is the true asset and treasure. That having fun is important. I'm different. I've changed. *I learned how to actually enjoy life with him.*

I'm kind of a guardian for the team. I think my main contribution is that I can step in if and when the team needs my help. I look for solutions when they need one. I look to bring assets to the table for them. Manuel calls me an "Advisor." How I feel is, "What do you guys need?" And then I apply any resources I have.

I'm not there every day but I'm always alert to what they need, and whether or not they need my help, and then I use everything at my disposal. At the end of the day, that's my family.

When you ask, "What do you think is Manuel's biggest accomplishment?" I think my answer is very different from most of the world.

He's got four children that adore him, that look up to him, that have experienced life at a very fun level because they have a life-loving, experience-loving father that cares about wanting to do something and wanting to do it with his kids. He may not know it yet, but he's got four amazing people that are his best product. His eldest son is an impeccable gentleman. That doesn't happen without an example. He's a lovely gentleman not only to his mother, but his grandmothers; they've had the best example of a man, of a parent, of a father, of a friend, through how he views and treats others. He's always admiring people. He loves powerhouses. He's always stood up for himself. He doesn't let people push him back. He always finds the solution in a playful good way. My kids can experience what a successful *person* looks like. Not a successful *businessperson*. He's a role model for the things they should be creating and how much to go after things in life. He's so highly productive and highly energetic. You have these four young creatures that are looking at that. They are *very* proud of him and completely in love with him. That drives him and motivates him. I believe it's his best accomplishment.

Marketing is not easy. It's a very competitive and very stressful job because sometimes you will find that clients expect you to be one hundred percent responsible for the income of their operation. It's more than just marketing. The result depends on your sales team, your service, and your product. Marketers get a lot of pressure to perform. You don't perform? You get fired. The pressure to be a marketer is a high standard all of the time. You have very little leeway with people's advertising dollars. If you can't withstand that constant pressure, don't do it. You always have to be on top of the trends, and it takes a certain type of person to do that. You have to admire the ones who can. It seems like anyone can do it.

The truth is they have to be keen to understand many things, the technology, the market. What I love about the team is that I am absolutely sure they are *highly* competent people. I understand the details of the degree of competence. It's not just anyone who got a degree from a university. You'll feel the pressure.

If you're still there and you like it, and you can deal with the pressure, that's great. Our team is absolutely up to the task. I get to use my own highly competent skills to do work that is very special. Just understanding that I respect that in others, especially in two amazing teams for AGM® and NaturalSlim®.

What one word best describes Manuel?

I have to say "Caring." Other than that… Relentless. Passionate. Intense. Energetic. Generous.

How do you manage to "do it all"?

From a personal perspective, the truth of the matter is you have to have support. If you pick the right people around you, and they are supportive and not a liability, you can do all the things. Choose the right spouse and make sure they are supportive, and that they don't in any way feel threatened by you doing anything. I get the opposite of any negativity from Manuel. I get cheerleading from him. Always. It's great if you have supportive parents as we both have had. Add to the team all the people who are supportive of the things you want to do. Now you have a true team.

What is the best advice you can give other husband and wife working teams?

I wouldn't give advice… that's not my method of operating… I believe in *not* giving advice to other marriages. No two marriages are alike, but you have to ask, "Does it work for me?" Understand what the other is doing in life and have that mutual support. I'm devoted to what Manuel wants to do. I'll voice my opinion. But we talk it out, and then we're both all in.

Devote yourself to the other person without putting yourself first. His success is my success. And his is mine. At least he makes me feel that way.

What's your favorite thing about Manuel?

Depends on the circumstances. He's so dynamic, so my favorite thing is that he is *my husband*. He's a very good, very easy-to-love guy. Easy to befriend. I think he also has a very sharp sense of when someone shouldn't be in our space or be our friend, and he won't go all in with that person. He'll get really passionate about people, but he also knows when to step back and walk away. I think that's his essence: connecting, but not without the ability to differentiate. He has great people skills. Smart people skills. He's an extremely good judge of character and able to spot amazing people... also able to know there are times to walk away.

***

So now you know quite a bit about not only Manuel but also the incredible team at Attention Grabbing Media®. As you might remember from an earlier chapter, the top lesson Manuel learned from his greatest mentor was the importance of building a team of people around you who can help you push forward the same purpose. Reading the answers from Manuel's team to my questions clearly demonstrates the power of having a dedicated team of ninjas aligned to the vision of one leader with an obsession to help and impact the lives of others. As Manuel himself would say… "Don't wait around for the perfect time. Build your own team of ninjas."

ACKNOWLEDGEMENTS

Honestly, without a few specific people in my life, I wouldn't be where I am today. And since I have always believed in giving credit where credit is due, I'd like to thank them here. Many people have been amazing allies along the way, so many that I couldn't possibly name them all, but in this dedication, you'll find the people who rise high in the story of my incredible journey. I dedicate this book to the wonderful people I had the honor of encountering along the way.

First and foremost, my deepest thanks to my father. As far back as I can recall, my father was my hero. During the darkest years of my life, he became my savior. He took me off the troubled path I was on, never gave up on me, and showed me the road to becoming a better human being. In later years, I had the privilege of playing the game of business side by side with him for many years. Every step of the way, I had the honor of learning from him what it was like to have a passion for helping and impacting others.

My father is the one who inspired me to strive to become one of the best marketers on this planet. He helped me understand that the real purpose of marketing was not to produce money, but to impact and help people with your message, products, and services and that by doing so, money would inevitably follow. He helped me understand what 'work ethic' *really* meant. I was able to witness and be part of that intense dedication right up until I lost him in 2021.

This book is wholeheartedly dedicated to him. He introduced me to a deep appreciation for curiosity and learning. He was instrumental in the creation of my marketing company, Attention Grabbing Media® (AGM®). From being my number one advisor and guide to being Attention Grabbing Media®'s first and most prominent client, over the years he became AGM®'s proudest accomplishment. The whole AGM® team is eternally grateful for him and how he inspired us with his never-ending motivation to change the world. My father's presence and influence will forever live among us.

"¡Porque la verdad siempre triunfa!"
(*Because the truth always triumphs!*)
Frank Suarez 1950 – 2021

I would like to also make a special mention to my stepmom Elizabeth for being my father's sidekick for over two decades and for always loving him and his family as her own.

I've also had several influential mentors along the way, who I'd like to mention here:

Especially:

Gary Vaynerchuk (founder of Vayner Media). Gary opened my eyes to the world of opportunities out there and gave me the mindset necessary to succeed in the game of business (and life) through his books and video education.

Ben Cummings (E-Commerce educator), another great marketing teacher, not only taught me how to be a professional marketer with his years of education but also opened doors to me no one else ever did. Those doors helped me discover that I had marketing magic in me.

Jason Fladlien ("The Webinar King") is a marketing legend and one of my first mentors. He was the one that got me started on my path to becoming a marketer when I purchased my first online marketing course from

> him. I consider him to be one of the greatest marketing minds alive.
>
> Grant Cardone (Entrepreneur and Social Media Influencer). Grant has shown me what it takes to make a massive impact in this world and has helped ignite a fire in me to push for greatness through his teachings and mindset.

There are also several incredible people who have allowed me to be part of their remarkable successes:

Dr. Eric Berg (a.k.a. "The Knowledge Doc" and creator of one of the largest health YouTube channels on the planet)

Nancy Cartwright (the voice of Bart Simpson, Chuckie Finster, and many other characters)

Chick Corea (the late giant jazz legend)

I would like to make a very special mention of my favorite philosopher, introduced to me by my father:

L. Ron Hubbard™ helped me understand what my true potential was. Through his teachings and philosophy, I was able to climb out of the darkness and step into the light. He presented me with a path to make myself better, stronger, and saner overall as a spiritual being. Without Mr. Hubbard's wisdom and advice, I would never have even started this wonderful adventure that has become my professional career.

Gratitude goes to my biggest source of daily inspiration: my four amazing children, Adrian, Camila, Julian, and Sofia. They are solely responsible for my initial push to survive, and they awakened in me a desire to create a life I could never have dreamed of before they came into my world.

I must mention here a very important person in my life, my mother. She was a warrior that fought for this family, her children and who has been one of my top fans every step of the way, always loving and supporting me, no matter how dark life became at times.

To my siblings Francisco, Gabriel, and Nicole: you helped mold me into a fierce competitor. You protected me, loved me, and took care of me during the darkest days we experienced as a family, and I am forever grateful for all of you. Nicole also helped me design the cover of this book to be exactly what I envisioned "Marketing Magic" to be.

I'd like to also mention Julianne (Jules) De Armon who is not only my cousin, but an expert in everything she does, including editing this book. With her help, I know I can deliver my message in such a way that not only impacts the lives of thousands but can be easily understood and applied.

Also, special thanks to Karen Nelson Bell, who helped with the inspiration for the structure of this book, as well as Arte Maren for his guidance and contribution to the design and content of this book.

To my Attention Grabbing Media® partners, the AGM® staff, and my NaturalSlim® staff – I wouldn't be where I am today without you. This group embodies the true definition of a team. I don't consider myself a *self-made* success. I am one hundred percent *team-made*, and I am what I am today because of the incredible partners and team members I have had the honor going into battle with every day.